I0393522

THE GRAYMOUSE FAMILY OF
FAMILY OF
WAINSCOT STREET

THE GRAYMOUSE FAMILY OF WAINSCOT STREET

Artist-Search Version

Flora Westcott Clere

Print information available on the last page.

Rev. date: 07/14/2016

To order additional copies of this book, contact:
Xlibris
1-888-795-4274
www.Xlibris.com
Orders@Xlibris.com

Or
www.aedok.com
544454

INTRODUCTION

GREETINGS TO ALL ILLUSTRATORS, PHOTOGRAPHERS, AND GRAPHIC DESIGNERS

AEDOK, the Archive For Education And Dissemination Of Knowledge.

In the **AEDOK** archives we discovered this delightful tale of the trials and tribulations of a family of "mouse folk". The story was in multiple drafts, of some disarray and incompleteness, so we edited it and completed it.

Now we need the artwork.

And we would like YOU to participate!

The completed work, *THE GRAYMOUSE FAMILY OF WAINSCOT STREET—PICTURE BOOK*, is to be approximately 70 pages, 34 of those pages (plus two for the front and back cover) will be PICTURE PAGES, pages containing pictures, artwork. Thirty-Six pieces of art.

AEDOK has decided to "search the world" for the artwork.

We are asking that you participate in **AEDOK**'s *THE GRAYMOUSE FAMILY OF WAINSCOT STREET—ARTIST SEARCH*, to find that artwork most appreciated by the viewers as judged by a counting of Internet votes[1]. The artist who's art receives the most votes thru the official **AEDOK** web site voting pages will be the selected artist who's art will be the artwork for *THE GRAYMOUSE FAMILY OF WAINSCOT STREET—PICTURE BOOK.*

What will this PICTURE BOOK look like?

It will be 8.5" x 11" pages, glossy, full color, soft cover. Our publisher for this PICTURE BOOK is *Xlibris* and you can go to their web site for examples of their work:

www.xlibris.com

But you, the artist participant in our project, will not be working with them, *Xlibris*, you will be working with us, **AEDOK**. This book you are reading explains the procedure and requirements.

And, although we can publish only ONE physical picture book at this time[2] so only ONE artist can be selected, there are no losers in this artist search.

[1]   Voting may be based upon both the individual pages and on the artwork as a whole. Anyone may vote as often as he likes as the artwork is posted and as new participants are involved. There is a $1 non-refundable processing fee per vote.

[2]   **AEDOK** will publish any artists work in his own *THE GRAYMOUSE FAMILY OF WAINSCOT STREET— PICTURE BOOK,* providing said artist pay **AEDOK** the full cost at that time. The current cost of physically publishing this single version of *THE GRAYMOUSE FAMILY OF WAINSCOT STREET - PICTURE BOOK,* is $1500. NOTE: **AEDOK** is NOT promoting the publication of your artwork in your own *THE GRAYMOUSE FAMILY OF WAINSCOT STREET - PICTURE BOOK.* **AEDOK** is NOT soliciting the $1500 from you. **AEDOK** makes NO claim that you would ever recover your investment. And remember, the CD version will be produced by **AEDOK** for each participant as part of the participation, for no additional cost.

Because, for EACH PARTICIPANT, *AEDOK* WILL CREATE A CD VERSION, *THE GRAYMOUSE FAMILY OF WAINSCOT STREET—CD VERSION— Artist Name*. We can do this because *AEDOK* does not need to pay an external source, a publisher, to create these CDs, whereas we must contract a publisher for the *PICTURE BOOK*.

The SINGLE *PICTURE BOOK* will be published thru *Xlibris* and distributed by *Xlibris* and their associates, available to the world for purchase at the various web sites.

The CD VERSIONS, one for EACH PARTICIPANT, will be published by *AEDOK* and distributed by *AEDOK*, available to the world for purchase at the *AEDOK* web site.

This may be historic. This may be the first time a book is published with ALL THE DIFFERENT VERSIONS of the art work presented. If there are 100 applicants, there will be 101 versions of this book. If there are 1000 applicants, there will be 1001 versions of this book.

THIS MAY BECOME A COLLECTOR'S ITEM. "BUY THEM ALL", as they say.

So, all your friends, family, and voters, and others, will be able to purchase a copy of YOUR version regardless of how your artwork eventually appears: paper or cd.

Now, about the version you are reading? This copy in your hands.

What you are reading is *THE GRAYMOUSE FAMILY OF WAINSCOT STREET—ARTIST SEARCH VERSION* which has the story book text exactly as it will appear in the PICTURE BOOK VERSION (even numbered pages), but in place of the PICTURE PAGES (odd numbered pages), we describe to you, the artist, what we envision the artwork to represent.

The book you are reading, this book, is physically smaller. The PICTURE BOOK will be 8.5" x 11" glossy, full color, soft cover. But the text of the story on page 2 of this book will be page 2 of the PICTURE BOOK. And page 4 and page 6 and so forth.

We have labeled each PICTURE PAGE according to the page number it will have in the book. For example PICTURE PAGE 3, PICTURE PAGE 5, PICTURE PAGE 7, and so forth. So, there is no PICTURE PAGE 4 because the even numbered pages are text of the story and odd numbered pages are the pictures for the story.

So, the thirty-fourth picture you provide will be page 69. Of course there are two more pictures for the covers.

FOR EACH PICTURE PAGE, WE HAVE SELECTED TEXT FROM THE STORY, USUALLY FROM THE FACING PAGE, AS A STARTING POINT FOR YOU, THE ARTIST, TO VISUALIZE. THE ACTUAL ART YOU PRODUCE WE LEAVE SOLELY TO YOU. WE SIMPLY SUGGEST THE TEXT AS A STARTING POINT.

If you think there is some image more pressing, or of more importance to present, that is up to you, but the quoted text is a good starting point.

THE FORMAT OF ALL PICTURE PAGES

You may want to go to book stores and libraries to examine other picture books and their artwork. You may devote the entire page to a single picture. You may split the picture in two. You may have multiple frames, say 4 or 6, like in comic strips and others showing action and progression.

What ever you think best allows you to present *your* art to illustrate our story.

Sometimes a single picture is best, sometimes a series of smaller pictures like a comic strip. You, the artist, make the decisions as how best to display your talent.

You may use captions for each, for some, for all, or for none. You may use "thought bubbles", or "speech bubbles", or other artistic tools. But you don't have to.

Single pictures often stand alone. Multiple pictures showing progression or action sometimes do, but sometimes don't have text bubbles, or captions. Again, up to you.

If you do use text, please quote text from the actual story. Do not make up text.

Also, you must submit only ONE 8.5" x 11" page for a single PICTURE PAGE. If your artwork is of multiple frames as discussed above, you must either draw it that way or YOU must do the cutting & pasting to produce a SINGLE, finished, page of art.

When this story is published with the selected art in the PICTURE BOOK, the pages will be 8.5" x 11" in full color. You decide how much color to use in your artwork.

The only restriction (aside from being morally and socially acceptable) is that EACH PICTURE PAGE WHICH YOU SUBMIT TO *AEDOK* BE A SINGLE 8.5" x 11" PAGE. Fully complete. Requiring no work on the part of *AEDOK*, save scanning it on our 8.5" x 11" scanner.

In other words, as just explained you may employ any techniques you desire but YOU must do all the cutting and pasting, if any, submitting, as we've said, just a single page for each PICTURE PAGE. Therefore you must submit 36 pages of artwork. That is, one for each PICTURE PAGE (34) plus one for the FRONT COVER and one for the BACK COVER. **Thirty-Six total pages of artwork.**

Why should you participate? It's a lot of work.

AEDOK makes no claims, warrants, or representations that you, the participant, shall recover your participation fee. AEDOK makes no claims, warrants, or representations that you, the participant, shall profit momentarily from your participation.

All participants should participate in order to show case their talents.

Having said that however, based upon the bonafide, non-refunded sales of the PICTURE BOOK or the CD's of the respective participants, for which **AEDOK** actually receives payment, **AEDOK** shall pay a $1 commission to the participant who's artwork was in the PICTURE BOOK or CD sold, subject to a contract to be signed. Payment made quarterly or as otherwise deemed by **AEDOK**.

This is our way of thanking you for helping us get this marvelous little children's tale out to the public with the VAST VARIETY of artwork you are going to provide!

At the back of this book is a participation agreement.

So, sit back, read the story, and visualize how YOU would illustrate *THE GRAYMOUSE FAMILY OF WAINSCOT STREET*.

We look forward to your participation.

August E. Drews
Editor

END OF INTRODUCTION

WHAT FOLLOWS NOW IS WHAT YOU SHOULD ENVISION THE BOOK TO BE.

THIS IS
PICTURE PAGE FRONT COVER

This page will be a single piece of artwork. It will be 8.5" x 11" glossy, full color. The information provided on this page is for assistance to you, the artist. It will not appear in the 8.5" x 11" full color Picture Book. This and every other page that is marked, "PICTURE PAGE", is to contain the appropriate piece of artwork from the selected artist.

THE THEME OF *THIS* PICTURE PAGE

AEDOK HAS NO IDEA HOW THE COVER SHOULD APPEAR.

It is totally up to you. For sometimes, a cover is a accurate depiction of the content and other times it too is a fiction, a montage or representation that, as they say, "takes liberty". Sometimes simple. Sometimes complex.

BUT REMEMBER. WE WANT THE CHILDREN AND THEIR PARENTS TO BE ATTRACTED TO THE BOOK.

You are the artist, you decide.

A participation form is at the back of this book. You may submit a photocopy if you don't want to damage this book to remove the form. Read the form, understand it, sign it, and enclose the participation fee. Or, enter online at

www.aedok.com/graymouseartsearch

Have fun. We look forward to receiving your creations.

THE GRAYMOUSE FAMILY OF WAINSCOT STREET

ARTIST-SEARCH
VERSION

by Flora Westcott Clare
edited by August E. Drews
illustrations by
YOU COULD BE THE ILLUSTRATOR

FOR DETAILS
SEE THE INTRODUCTION
AND
SEE ANY OF THE PAGES LABELED
"PICTURE-PAGE"

A PARTICIPATION FORM CAN BE FOUND
AT THE END OF THIS BOOK
OR
www.aedok.com/graymouseartsearch

CHAPTER 1

No longer than the day before yesterday, and no further away than from here to there, in a comfortable *old mousehouse on Wainscot Street* in Kitchentown, there lived . . . until they all moved out so they could move into a safer place . . . the very nice family of mousefolk named Graymouse.

In this family there is Grandpa Graymouse and Grandma Graymouse; Papa Graymouse and Mama Graymouse; and four Graymouse children: three little Graymouse girls and one little Graymouse boy.

The little Graymouse girls are triplets. Their birthdays come all on the same day. They are so much alike, no one outside the Graymouse family can tell one from the other. They're named Ee-nie, Me-nie, and Mi-nie. The little Graymouse boy's birthday is on a different day. He's the youngest of the Graymouse family and his name is Mo.

You may think Ee-nie, Me-nie, Mi-nie, and Mo are queer names even for Graymouses but Mamma Graymouse doesn't think that way. She named her children Ee-nie, Me-nie, Mi-nie, and Mo so that she could call them all at one time and all in one breath and their names would make a happy jingly sound . . . "Ee-nie, Me-nie, Mi-nie, Mo!" that's the way she generally calls them. But sometimes, because she is fond of jingly sounds, she uses three more breaths and adds to her call: "Catch a Meow by the toe; If he hollers let him go; Ee-nie, Me-nie, Mi-nie, Mo!"

Not that Mamma Graymouse ever expects any one of her children to ever attempt to catch a Meow by any part of his body. Oh no. Meows are enormous creatures compared to mousefolk and the worst enemy they have. In fact it is extremely dangerous for a Graymouse to get within pouncing distance of a Meow at any time. Just for fun Mamma Graymouse would call "Catch a Meow by the toe." She thought her children remembered what she had taught them when they were tiny mouse-babies—always if possible to keep a mouse-mile away from Meows. Over and over she told them that even though they couldn't see a Meow

2

THIS IS
PICTURE PAGE 3

The information provided on this page will not appear in the 8.5" x 11" full color Picture Book. This page will be a single piece of artwork. It will be 8.5" x 11" glossy, full color.

THE THEME OF *THIS* PICTURE PAGE
Hall and Wainscot

AEDOK recommends the theme of this PICTURE PAGE be based upon this text from the previous page:

mousehouse on Wainscot Street

AEDOK envisions an image of the inside of a human's house with a hallway and wainscot. We envision a mouse hole cut into the wainscot.

You can decide whether there is a mouse nose sticking out, whether there is a cat lurking in the background or whether that hideous image is saved until later, whether there are mouse tracks in this picture or later, what the furniture looks like. You are the artist, you decide.

A participation form is in back. You may submit a photo-copy. Read, understand, sign, and enclose the participation fee. Or, enter online at

www.aedok.com/graymouseartsearch

Have fun. We look forward to receiving your creations.

they could be pretty sure one was somewhere near if they happened to smell even a tiny whiff of catnip, for catnip is a weed all Meows are fond of chewing. "Run," she often said, "run like all-get-out to a hide-away and stay there safe while you smell the smell of catnip on the air."

Now like all children, the Graymouse children sometimes remember what they are told and sometimes they do not. But the Graymouses've been told often enough so that they should know that when Mamma Graymouse calls Ee-nie, Me-nie, Mi-nie, Mo; Catch a Meow by the toe; If he hollers let him go; Ee-nie, Me-nie, Mi-nie, Mo!", she calls all this only because she likes the rhyme and rhythm in its sound.

If Ee-nie, Me-nie, Mi-nie, and Mo *had* remembered on the day before the day before yesterday, this story might never have been written, but because they must have forgotten on that day, and because all the Graymouses have this peculiar idea of dressing, what happened happened.

What peculiar idea of dressing? Graymouses go about barefoot but at the same time wear a gray fur coat tightly zippered about their little bodies. Spring or summer, fall or winter, no one has ever seen a Graymouse going here, there, or anywhere, without his fur coat. *Nor has anyone ever seen any covering on a Graymouse's foot . . . not even a sandal to keep his toes from frost-bite in winter or his heal from stone-bruises in summer. As the Graymouses use their front feet when they wash their faces and lift up their food, they might sensibly leave these bare but cover their back feet.* But they don't. They just let every one of their tiny toes on their front feet and their back feet spread out and make dib-dab toe tracks wherever they travel. And because they didn't cover their feet, but on the day before the day before yesterday left dib-dab toe tracks in the dust of Kitchentown, what happened did happen. This story tells what, and how, and when, and where.

THIS IS
PICTURE PAGE 5

The information provided on this page will not appear in the 8.5" x 11" full color Picture Book. This page will be a single piece of artwork. It will be 8.5" x 11" glossy, full color.

THE THEME OF *THIS* PICTURE PAGE
Graymouse Washing and Eating

AEDOK recommends the theme of this PICTURE PAGE be based upon this text from the previous page:

> *Nor has anyone ever seen any covering on a Graymouse's foot . . . not even a sandal to keep his toes from frost-bite in winter or his heal from stone-bruises in summer. As the Graymouses use their front feet when they wash their faces and lift up their food, they might sensibly leave these bare but cover their back feet.*

You are the artist, you decide.

A participation form is in back. You may submit a photo-copy. Read, understand, sign, and enclose the participation fee. Or, enter online at

www.aedok.com/graymouseartsearch

Have fun. We look forward to receiving your creations.

CHAPTER 2

All the mouse-day of the day before the day before yesterday the Graymouse family spent going in and out of their round doorway on Wainscot Street. This way and that way they went: To the Pantry Shop at one corner of Wainscot Street for food; To Dribble Drop Falls on Sink Ridge at the other corner of the street for refreshing drinks of water when they were thirsty. They made so many trips, this way and that, that the dib-dab toe tracks cris-crossed at their doorway and Wainscot Street was messed up quite a bit with them. Those dib-dab toe marks were as plane as the nose on your face on the following mouse-morning.

It was a wonderful mouse-morning, that mouse-morning the day before yesterday. *Papa Graymouse had just come back from the mousehouse doorway and said so to Grandpa Graymouse who was peacefully reading the Squeak News in his easy chair in the living room of the mousehouse. Mamma Graymouse was bustling around in a terrific hurry getting breakfast ready. Ee-nie, Me-nie, Mi-nie, and Mo . . . looking like four huge gray caterpillars in their fur coats, so chubby you have to look closely to see their pink snubs of noses, their very round stick-up ears, and the very long slender tails hitched to their rear ends just exactly like all other Graymouses have . . . were running around and around in the center of the living room floor trying to grab their own tails and thereby beat themselves at their favorite game of Chase Your Tail.* Grandma Graymouse was not yet out of bed. She is a frail Graymouse and suffers from misery in her leg joints and is deaf in one ear. Every mouse-morning before she can budge a foot out of bed, she has to have three cheese crumbs to cure what ails her. As soon as she swallows the cheese, the misery goes out of her leg-joints—until the next mouse-night— she gets out of bed, and for the rest of the mouse-day can go wherever the rest of the Graymouse family goes and without the least bit of pain or trouble . . . although she still can hear only half of what is said to her.

THIS IS
PICTURE PAGE 7

The information provided on this page will not appear in the 8.5" x 11" full color Picture Book. This page will be a single piece of artwork. It will be 8.5" x 11" glossy, full color.

THE THEME OF *THIS* PICTURE PAGE
Family Activities

AEDOK recommends the theme of this PICTURE PAGE be based upon this text from the previous page:

> *Papa Graymouse had just come back from the mousehouse doorway and said so to Grandpa Graymouse who was peacefully reading the Squeak News in his easy chair in the living room of the mousehouse. Mamma Graymouse was bustling around in a terrific hurry getting breakfast ready. Ee-nie, Me-nie, Mi-nie, and Mo . . . looking like four huge gray caterpillars in their fur coats, so chubby you have to look closely to see their pink snubs of noses, their very round stick-up ears, and the very long slender tails hitched to their rear ends just exactly like all other Graymouses have . . . were running around and around in the center of the living room floor trying to grab their own tails and thereby beat themselves at their favorite game of Chase Your Tail.*

You are the artist, you decide.

A participation form is in back. You may submit a photo-copy. Read, understand, sign, and enclose the participation fee. Or, enter online at

www.aedok.com/graymouseartsearch

Have fun. We look forward to receiving your creations.

When Papa Graymouse said it was a wonderful mouse-morning he also said the sun was all the way down and the moon was all the way up and Wainscot Street was full of shadow spots so it would be safe for them all to go marketing early. You see, the Graymouses like to travel in shadows.

When Ee-nie, Me-nie, and Mi-nie heard Papa Graymouse say they could go marketing early . . . marketing was what the little Graymouse children liked best to do . . . they stopped turning around like four tops in the middle of the floor and let out a number of woopie squeaks of joy. Marketing early! Marketing early! Marketing early!

Of course none of the Graymouses knew that just at that time a huge Meow was hurrying through Kitchentown on his way to Over Beyond where he had planned to take a snooze. Though he hurried, his tread was soft, for his sharp claws were drawn back into his cushiony feet which he put down carefully, one before the other. His enormous green eyes were rolling from side to side in his head and his powerful tail was lashing this way and that with a hissing, s-wish-h-h, s-w-ish-h-h, swish! swoosh!

Suddenly as he came onto Wainscot Street, the Meow stopped so short, his four cushiony feet skidded together. He had seen the dib-dab toe marks made by the Graymouse family.

"What's this I am seeing?", he said down under his breath and down went his nose to take a sniff. "Mouse tracks", he answered himself all excited, "And fresh!" Sniff, sniff, sniff he went, right along a line of those mouse tracks until he had sniffed right up to the mousehouse doorway where they cris-crossed as they went in and out. There he stopped stock still, lifted his head, and listened.

And as bad luck for the Graymouse family would have it, he heard Ee-nie, Me-nie, Mi-nie, and Mo letting out their most joyous "Squeak! Squeak! Squeak!"—To market Early! Early! Early!

Down on his haunches right before the mousehouse doorway the Meow sat himself and raising his head in the air let out a long drawn-out yowl, "Me-me-me-ow-oW-OW-MEOW!" The Meow wanted to catch a Graymouse and they were all inside the mousehouse—that's why he yowled. *The yowl started far down in his throat but rose higher and higher and came out of his mouth louder and louder until it penetrated right through the mousehouse doorway, bumped from pillar to post along the*

THIS IS
PICTURE PAGE 9

The information provided on this page will not appear in the 8.5" x 11" full color Picture Book. This page will be a single piece of artwork. It will be 8.5" x 11" glossy, full color.

THE THEME OF *THIS* PICTURE PAGE
Meow Discovers Dib-Dab Toe Marks

AEDOK recommends the theme of this PICTURE PAGE be based upon this text from the previous page:

> *"What's this I am seeing?", he said down under his breath and down went his nose to take a sniff. "Mouse tracks", he answered himself all excited,*

You are the artist, you decide.

A participation form is in back. You may submit a photo-copy. Read, understand, sign, and enclose the participation fee. Or, enter online at

www.aedok.com/graymouseartsearch

Have fun. We look forward to receiving your creations.

zig-zag hall that led to the Graymouse living room, and burst right around the Graymouses, and they were so frightened not one of them moved. The sound of the yowl faded. For a second the mousehouse was still . . . almost as still as though it was plumb full of nothing but nothingness.

Then heavenly mouse-day! From her bed in a far corner of the living room Grandma Graymouse's voice cut through the silence. "Cheese! Cheese! Cheese!" came her wispy voice. "I want my cheese crumbs so I can get out of bed."

This mouse-morning of all mouse-mornings no one had yet taken Grandma Graymouse her cheese crumbs. And as she had her good ear tucked tightly in the folds of her pillow, she hadn't heard the Meow's yowl and had no idea that a terrible danger threatened the Graymouse family.

As was to be expected, the Meow, still on his haunches outside the mousehouse doorway lifting first one of his big cushiony feet and then the other to examine the sharpness of his claws, heard *Grandma Graymouse squeak, "Cheese! Cheese! Cheese!", and let out another of his blood-curdling yowls, "me-me-me-mE-OW-OW-OW-OW!"* It was a yowl of impatience—he couldn't get what he wanted. And again, Grandma Graymouse not hearing the Meow's yowl squeaked, "Cheese! Cheese! Cheese! I want my cheese crumbs!" And that's the way they went: First the yowl and then the squeak. Until Grandma Graymouse's voice grew whispier and whispier, and the yowl grew louder and louder! Then all was silent again.

Grandpa Graymouse was the first to speak out in the quiet. "Yes, yes, Grandma Graymouse. Right away, right away," he called and every other Graymouse's head turned in his direction. "There's no reason for us to be all shushed up," was what Grandpa Graymouse squeaked. "There's no better hideaway than our mousehouse. How could a Meow get through our doorway?"

"You're right, you're always right," squeaked back Papa Graymouse, "There's nothing to be afraid of while we stay inside the mousehouse but it's as much as a Graymouse's life is worth to venture out."

The other Graymouses heaved signs of relief and before Grandma Graymouse could call out again, Mo squeaked, "I'll tell Grandma Graymouse I'll get her cheese."

THIS IS
PICTURE PAGE II

The information provided on this page will not appear in the 8.5" x 11" full color Picture Book. This page will be a single piece of artwork. It will be 8.5" x 11" glossy, full color.

THE THEME OF *THIS* PICTURE PAGE
Yowl and Cheese Demand

AEDOK recommends the theme of this PICTURE PAGE be based upon this text from the previous page:

> *The yowl started far down in his throat but rose higher and higher and came out of his mouth louder and louder until it penetrated right through the mousehouse doorway, bumped from pillar to post along the zig-zag hall that led to the Graymouse living room, and burst right around the Graymouses,*

> . . .

> *Grandma Graymouse squeak, "Cheese! Cheese! Cheese!", and let out another of his blood-curdling yowls, "me-me-me-mE-OW-OW-OW-OW!"*

You are the artist, you decide.

A participation form is in back. You may submit a photo-copy. Read, understand, sign, and enclose the participation fee. Or, enter online at

www.aedok.com/graymouseartsearch

Have fun. We look forward to receiving your creations.

"Don't tell her about the Meow," warned Grandpa Graymouse, "What she doesn't know won't hurt her."

Mo stopped at Grandma Graymouse's bedside and whispered in her good ear. She settled back peacefully on her pillow and Mo scampered into the storeroom were the supplies of food were kept. Ee-nie, Me-nie, and Mi-nie ran to help Mamma Graymouse put the bowls of corn porridge on the table. Grandpa Graymouse went back to his newspaper reading. And Papa Graymouse disappeared down the long zig-zag hall. *He wanted to get an eyeful of this Meow and find out why the yowls had stopped, who by now could be heard parading up and down in front of their doorway. Soon he came running back.*

"It's the largest Meow I've ever laid my eyes on." he said. "He's colored like the marmalade in the glass jar in the Pantry Shop, brown and orange stripes from one end of him to the other."

"Lucky we did plenty of marketing while we had the chance. We won't have to go hungry while we wait for him to go one his way."

"Don't be so sure about that," said Grandpa Graymouse as they all settled down to breakfast, "Now that this Meow has found our doorway, he's going to be waiting there for a long, long, time. I see nothing for us to do but to move to another mousehouse far away from Wainscot Street. I don't mean to stay there always . . . Just long enough for the Meow to forget us."

"But there's only one way out of the mousehouse and that's onto Wainscot Street," wailed Mamma Graymouse.

"Only one way out to the Pantry Shop for food," cried Ee-nie, Me-nie, and Mi-nie all together, their mouths full of corn porridge.

"Now, now," soothed Grandpa Graymouse, "Don't worry. We've always needed another going-out doorway. Already there's a crack in our back wall. Papa Graymouse and I will make that into a doorway onto Rubbish Lane. And the quickest way will be by Sharp-Tooth Gnaw."

Papa Graymouse nodded his head. "There's no time to lose and no way as good as the old-fashioned Graymouse way of making openings. Let's get started." And away he and Grandpa Graymouse

THIS IS
PICTURE PAGE 13

The information provided on this page will not appear in the 8.5" x 11" full color Picture Book. This page will be a single piece of artwork. It will be 8.5" x 11" glossy, full color.

THE THEME OF *THIS* PICTURE PAGE
Papa Graymouse In Terror

AEDOK recommends the theme of this PICTURE PAGE be based upon this text from the previous page:

> *He wanted to get an eyeful of this Meow and find out why the yowls had stopped, who by now could be heard parading up and down in front of their doorway. Soon he came running back.*
>
> *"It's the largest Meow I've ever laid my eyes on." he said. "He's colored like the marmalade in the glass jar in the Pantry Shop, brown and orange stripes from one end of him to the other."*

You are the artist, you decide.

A participation form is in back. You may submit a photo-copy. Read, understand, sign, and enclose the participation fee. Or, enter online at

www.aedok.com/graymouseartsearch

Have fun. We look forward to receiving your creations.

went to the back of the mousehouse. *Soon one was gnawing the wood on one side of the crack in the back wall and the other was gnawing the wood on the other side of the crack in the back wall.* Before that mouse-day was over, that mousehouse would have a new doorway.

Then Mamma Graymouse had time to think of Mo and the cheese crumbs for Grandma Graymouse who seemed to have fallen asleep again. She looked at Ee-nie, Me-nie, and Mi-nie, "Whatever makes Mo so slow about those cheese crumbs he went after? Go and see what he's up to." Off to the store room the three little Graymouse girls scampered as fast as their legs would carry them. There was Mo in the middle of the storeroom floor holding the cheese box.

"Grandma Graymouse want's her cheese crumbs right away," squeaked Ee-nie, Me-nie, and Mi-nie all together and it sounded just like one big squeak.

"But I can't bring the cheese crumbs," said Mo, "There isn't any cheese in the box." And he held out the empty box for them to see. "And there isn't any in the storeroom. I've looked everywhere."

"No cheese for Grandma Graymouse!" sobbed Ee-nie, Me-nie, and Mi-nie and great gobby tears trinkled out of their eyes and dropped off the ends of their noses. "If Grandma Graymouse doesn't get her cheese crumbs she won't be able to walk and then we'll have to stay in this mousehouse with her until there is no food and we'll get hungrier and hungrier and maybe starve . . ."

Their mournful wail was cut short by a sharp call from Mamma Graymouse and this time there was no rhyme or jingle in the sound, "Ee-nie, Me-nie, Mi-nie, and Mo!"

Out of the storeroom the children ran pell-mell. That sharp call meant to get to her quickly.

"There wasn't any cheese in the cheese box," cried Mo when he was near her. "I searched every corner of the storeroom and didn't find even a snippet of cheese anywhere."

Mamma Graymouse gasped out, "No cheese?" She couldn't believe her own ears. "However could we have been so forgetful? No cheese and no way to get to the Pantry Shop. I don't know what to give Grandma Graymouse in place of the cheese we haven't got."

"It'll have to be something strong," said Ee-nie.

THIS IS
PICTURE PAGE 15

The information provided on this page will not appear in the 8.5" x 11" full color Picture Book. This page will be a single piece of artwork. It will be 8.5" x 11" glossy, full color.

THE THEME OF *THIS* PICTURE PAGE
Gnawing

AEDOK recommends the theme of this PICTURE PAGE be based upon this text from the previous page:

> *Soon one was gnawing the wood on one side of the crack in the back wall and the other was gnawing the wood on the other side of the crack in the back wall.*

You are the artist, you decide.

A participation form is in back. You may submit a photo-copy. Read, understand, sign, and enclose the participation fee. Or, enter online at

www.aedok.com/graymouseartsearch

Have fun. We look forward to receiving your creations.

"So she can step lively," said Me-nie.

"And not totter along when we move to the new mousehouse," said Mi-nie.

Mo just stood and looked in wonder. He hadn't heard about the planned move to another mousehouse.

"I'll brew Grandma Graymouse some boneset tea," said Mamma Graymouse. And down from a hook in the ceiling she took a bunch of dried boneset leaves which she soon had boiling in a skillet of water. It was a tea *her* grandmother had often used for all sorts of ills. When she decided the strength from the leaves had boiled into the water, she poured the water into Grandma Graymouse's favorite blue bowl and carried it to Grandma Graymouse's bedside. Grandma Graymouse was now awake.

"Drink this, Grandma Graymouse," said Mamma Graymouse, "It's hot boneset tea and good for what ails you."

"Boneset tea?!" wailed Grandma Graymouse wobbling her head about on her pillow until her lace nightcap fell down over her eyes. "Boneset tea is bitter. I won't drink a drop of it. I want cheese, Cheese, CHEESE!"

Mamma Graymouse felt of Grandma Graymouse's nose. It felt hot. "She's feverish," she said to Ee-nie, Me-nie, Mi-nie, and Mo hovering at the bedside. "Perhaps she'll drink it if you ask her."

"Oh, Grandma Graymouse, please drink the boneset tea," begged Ee-nie, Me-nie, Mi-nie, and Mo all at once. So Grandma Graymouse did. But the boneset tea didn't do her any good at all. She tried her knee-joints. They still creaked. She tried to budge out of bed. She couldn't get out of bed no matter how hard she tried. Her nose was roasty-hot and her feet were frosty cold and Mamma Graymouse grew more worried and more worried for all Grandma Graymouse would say was, "Cheese, Cheese, Cheese." And the mousehouse was filled with the steady gnawing of Grandpa Graymouse and Papa Graymouse at the crack. It takes a long time to gnaw a doorway. The Meow was now parading from the Pantry Shop to Sink Ridge and every time he passed the mousehouse doorway on Wainscot Street he let out a terrifying meow, meow, meow, meow, "ME-e-e-e-e-e-e E-O-O-W!!!" No wonder . . . no wonder Mamma Graymouse completely forgot herself and said to Grandma Graymouse, "There isn't a morsel of cheese in the house, Grandma Graymouse."

THIS IS
PICTURE PAGE 17

The information provided on this page will not appear in the 8.5" x 11" full color Picture Book. This page will be a single piece of artwork. It will be 8.5" x 11" glossy, full color.

THE THEME OF *THIS* PICTURE PAGE
Fever

AEDOK recommends the theme of this PICTURE PAGE be based upon this text from the previous page:

> *Mamma Graymouse felt of Grandma Graymouse's nose. It felt hot. "She's feverish,"*

You are the artist, you decide.

A participation form is in back. You may submit a photo-copy. Read, understand, sign, and enclose the participation fee. Or, enter online at

www.aedok.com/graymouseartsearch

Have fun. We look forward to receiving your creations.

"Then send to the Pantry Shop for some," insisted Grandma Graymouse.

"There isn't a smitch of cheese in the Pantry Shop either," Mamma Graymouse told her.

At that Ee-nie, Me-nie, Mi-nie, and Mo looked at Mamma Graymouse, their eyes wide with astonishment, and Mamma Graymouse hurried them away from the bedside.

"Go and amuse yourselves in the corner," she said as she shooed them before her. "I'll find something for Grandma Graymouse to eat in place of the cheese crumbs."

"There *is* cheese in the Pantry Shop," Mo told her in a low-down whisper. "There always is a big yellow cheese on the middle shelf. And it was there the last time I was there."

"I know, I know," whispered back Mamma Graymouse. "I know the cheese is there but we can't get it. And we can't upset her more by telling her a fierce Meow is waiting outside our doorway to grab the first one of us that ventures out on Wainscot Street."

Ee-nie, Me-nie, Mi-nie, and Mo obediently went to their corner but they were too distressed by Grandma Graymouse's pitiful cries of, "Cheese! Cheese! Cheese!", though they knew that *Mamma Graymouse was giving her a spoonful of this and a spoonful of that and even trying onion poultices on her back feet to try to draw the fever out from her head.*

THIS IS
PICTURE PAGE 19

The information provided on this page will not appear in the 8.5" x 11" full color Picture Book. This page will be a single piece of artwork. It will be 8.5" x 11" glossy, full color.

THE THEME OF *THIS* PICTURE PAGE
Poultices

AEDOK recommends the theme of this PICTURE PAGE be based upon this text from the previous page:

> *Mamma Graymouse was giving her a spoonful of this and a spoonful of that and even trying onion poultices on her back feet to try to draw the fever out from her head.*

We think it'd be neat to see Grandma in bed under covers with her feet sticking out at the end, if that has not already been portrayed.

You are the artist, you decide.

A participation form is in back. You may submit a photo-copy. Read, understand, sign, and enclose the participation fee. Or, enter online at

www.aedok.com/graymouseartsearch

Have fun. We look forward to receiving your creations.

CHAPTER 3

"Have you given Grandma Graymouse spoonfuls of this and that?" asked Papa Graymouse.

Mamma Graymouse nodded. "And I have a cold bag on her head and hot onion poultices on both her hind feet. It's supposed to be a good way to draw the fever from her nose and carry it out through her heals. But I must say, it hasn't done the least bit of good."

"Well," said Papa Graymouse, "Grandma Graymouse is too heavy to carry. And we won't leave her in this house alone to starve to death. So we better get busy, thinking what to do." He sat down with his head in his hands, and Mama and Grandpa Graymouse sat down and put their heads in their hands: in the latest approved way for mouse-thinking. And there they sat, and sat, and sat, close in front of the newly created back door, trying to think of something, and saying under their breaths, "What can we do to make Grandma Graymouse strong without her dose of cheese crumbs?"

After they had been sitting like that for a while, mumbling the words over and over and not being able to make up their minds to anything, Ee-nie said, "I know what I'd do."

"What?" asked Me-nie, Mi-ne, and Mo.

"If I had said I'd get Grandma Graymouse her cheese I'd get it," said Ee-nie and she looked straight at Mo. "I'd go right this minute to the Pantry Shop and fetch her three little morsels of cheese. No Meow could stop me . . . if I'd said I'd get them."

"I was just making up my mind to go," said Mo, "only maybe Mamma wouldn't want me to."

"Maybe she wouldn't," said Ee-nie, "but you don't have to tell her do you? You could run out and get to the Pantry Shop in two shakes of a tail, Mo. You're awfully brave. That's because you're a boy."

"If I were a mouse-boy I'd be brave too," said Me-nie.

THIS IS
PICTURE PAGE 21

The information provided on this page will not appear in the 8.5" x 11" full color Picture Book. This page will be a single piece of artwork. It will be 8.5" x 11" glossy, full color.

THE THEME OF *THIS* PICTURE PAGE
Children Mice Planning

AEDOK recommends the theme of this PICTURE PAGE be based upon this text from the previous page:

> *"If I had said I'd get Grandma Graymouse her cheese I'd get it,"*
> *said Ee-nie and she looked straight at Mo.*

You are the artist, you decide.

A participation form is in back. You may submit a photo-copy. Read, understand, sign, and enclose the participation fee. Or, enter online at

www.aedok.com/graymouseartsearch

Have fun. We look forward to receiving your creations.

"It'll be a perilous adventure," declared Mo. "If the Meow catches me I'll probably be gobbled up in one gulp and you'll never see me again."

"You're so little he'll never see you," said Ee-nie.

"You better ask Grandma if cheese crumbs will surely make her strong and spry before you venture out," suggested Me-nie.

"I'm going to ask her if one cheese crumb will make her better. Maybe I won't be able to fetch any more because I'm only a little mouse-boy after all. But really I'm not afraid. If Grandma says, 'Yes', I'll start right away."

Softly Mo crept to Grandma Graymouse's bed. "Raise up your good hearing ear, Grandma Graymouse," he coaxed. "Would one little crumb of cheese make you well, Grandma Graymouse?"

Grandma Graymouse's head bobbed up from her pillow so quickly you'd have thought she had a spring in her back like a jack-in-the-box. "It would make me as fit as a fiddle, Mo," she said.

Of course she wouldn't have said that if she had known about the Meow but nobody had told her about him and she hadn't heard his yowls . . . so how could she know?

"You're quite sure you could walk fast and go a long way, if you had to maybe, if you had just one crumb of cheese?" Mo persisted, hoping Grandma Graymouse would change her mind and say no.

But Grandma Graymouse didn't say no. She said, "I could walk faster and farther than I've ever walked if I had just a little mite of cheese."

"Then I'll fetch you as many crumbs as I can carry," promised Mo.

And back to where Ee-nie, Me-nie, and Mi-nie were waiting close together in a huddle and he repeated to them what Grandma Graymouse had said.

"We've been making up our minds, while you were talking to Grandma Graymouse," said Ee-ni, "and we've decided to go to the Pantry Shop with you.

Inside himself Mo was glad when he heard Ee-nie, Me-nie, and Mi-nie say they would go to the Pantry Shop with him for he was quite jittery about going there all alone, but aloud to show what a brave boy he was he said, "You don't have to go with me. *I'm not afraid to go by myself. Girls will be a botheration on such a dangerous adventure." He insisted for a moment but thinking that Ee-nie, Me-nie, and Mi-nie were about to change their minds and not go with him, he hurried to add,* "If you insist I'll let you come along."

THIS IS
PICTURE PAGE 23

The information provided on this page will not appear in the 8.5" x 11" full color Picture Book. This page will be a single piece of artwork. It will be 8.5" x 11" glossy, full color.

THE THEME OF *THIS* PICTURE PAGE
Bragging Mo

AEDOK recommends the theme of this PICTURE PAGE be based upon this text from the previous pagr:

> I'm not afraid to go by myself. Girls will be a botheration on such a dangerous adventure." He insisted for a moment but thinking that Ee-nie, Me-nie, and Mi-nie were about to change their minds and not go with him, he hurried to add, "If you insist

You are the artist, you decide.

A participation form is in back. You may submit a photo-copy. Read, understand, sign, and enclose the participation fee. Or, enter online at

www.aedok.com/graymouseartsearch

Have fun. We look forward to receiving your creations.

"We insist! We insist! We insist!" squeaked Ee-nie, Me-nie, and Mi-nie, and were so anxious to go that Mo dared warn them, "I'll take a lot of courage. We'll have to get out of the doorway and into the shadow of Wainscot Street while the Meow's back is turned. I'll peek out of the doorway and when the Meow has passed our doorway and is on the way to Dribble Drop Falls corner, I'll rush out first. The three of you must come creeping silently behind me and turn every once in a while to keep watch of the Meow. I won't know what's going on in back of me for I'll be using my eyes to see what's going on in front. Let out a piercing squeak if he starts to trail us. That'll be our signal to rush for a hide-away. If he doesn't trail us we'll scamper as fast as we can into the Pantry Shop. And if we go fast enough we'll get there before the Meow turns around. Let's get going."

One behind the other, first Mo then Ee-nie, then Me-nie then Mi-nie, they crept softly from the living room and kept on creeping down the long zig-zag hall until they reached the doorway onto Wainscot Street. There they paused while Mo peeked out. And all he could see was the back of the Meow pacing up toward Dribble Drop Falls.

"Now's our chance," whispered Mo and out they sneaked into Wainscot Street, one at a time. Once outside, Oh, how they ran . . . almost as fast as the wind blows. In no time at all they were inside the Pantry Shop gasping for breath. Things were going so well they forgot their fears entirely.

"We made it," said Mo. "It was easy."

"The old Meow never saw us," said Ee-nie.

"He'll never suspect we're where we are," said Me-nie.

"He'll think we're in the mousehouse where we were," said Mi-nie.

But that's where Ee-nie, Me-nie, Mi-nie, and Mo fooled themselves.

On reaching Dribble Drop Falls the Meow had turned on his heal and started his parade back past the mousehouse doorway and on to the Pantry Shop. *Then his rolling green eyes caught sight of the new teeny-tiny dib-dab toe marks just made. Down went his head and his nose sniffed in the toe-mark smell.*

THIS IS
PICTURE PAGE 25

The information provided on this page will not appear in the 8.5" x 11" full color Picture Book. This page will be a single piece of artwork. It will be 8.5" x 11" glossy, full color.

THE THEME OF *THIS* PICTURE PAGE
The Meow Again

AEDOK recommends the theme of this PICTURE PAGE be based upon this text from the previous page:

> *Then his rolling green eyes caught sight of the new teeny-tiny dib-dab toe marks just made. Down went his head and his nose sniffed in the toe-mark smell.*

You are the artist, you decide.

A participation form is in back. You may submit a photo-copy. Read, understand, sign, and enclose the participation fee. Or, enter online at

www.aedok.com/graymouseartsearch

Have fun. We look forward to receiving your creations.

"Mouse-children's toe marks . . . made while my back was turned . . . and leading right to the Pantry Shop. Yum! Yum! Juicy and licking his chops, his green eyes glowing like green lights, the Meow stepped silently but quickly along the new toe-marks trail. Neither Ee-nie nor Me-nie, Mi-nie nor Mo expected the Meow was doing what he was doing.

"Let's hurry and get the cheese crumbs for Grandma Graymouse," Mo was saying, leading the way along a shelf crowded with dishes. He went so fast that soon he had outdistanced Ee-nie, Me-nie, and Mi-nie and disappeared around a bulging stack of dinner plates.

Ee-nie, Me-nie, and Mi-nie had not noticed that they were alone for Mi-nie had just noted a delicious smell. "Like . . . cinnamon buns," she remarked.

"That's just what it smells like," said Ee-nie and Me-nie and the three of them lifted their little pink noses and wiggled them about to get the spicy sweet fragrance.

"And there it is!" Me-nie pointed to a plate of buns nearby.

"So it is," said Ee-nie, "and it's just what Mi-nie thought it was, sugar-frosted cinnamon buns. We aught to take a wee nibble."

And so they did. They each took one nibble. And then they each took two nibbles. And after that they stopped counting the nibbles . . . and just went on nibbling as fast as they could.

Mo, who thought they were close behind him . . . that's the way they had promised to travel . . . kept going ahead but carefully to make sure he didn't bump into anything. When he noticed that he could no longer hear them, he stretched out his long slender tail and felt about with its sensitive tip. No Ee-nie, Me-nie, or Mi-nie could he feel. "They've stopped on the way," he told himself and left me to go on after the cheese crumbs alone." And so he did. He went on until he came to the great round yellow cheese on the middle shelf. A three-corner piece was all that had been cut out of it. Into the opening space where the piece had been, stepped Mo. On each side of him rose walls of yellow richness soft as butter.

"My! My! Won't Grandma Graymouse like this!" he thought as deep into it he sank his two sharp front teeth. Sinking his teeth this way and that

THIS IS
PICTURE PAGE 27

The information provided on this page will not appear in the 8.5" x 11" full color Picture Book. This page will be a single piece of artwork. It will be 8.5" x 11" glossy, full color.

THE THEME OF *THIS* PICTURE PAGE
Mo's Tail, Others Nibbling

AEDOK recommends the theme of this PICTURE PAGE be based upon this text from the previous page:

> *And so they did. They each took one nibble. And then they each took two nibbles. And after that they stopped counting the nibbles . . . and just went on nibbling as fast as they could.*
>
> *Mo, who thought they were close behind him . . . that's the way they had promised to travel . . . kept going ahead but carefully to make sure he didn't bump into anything. When he noticed that he could no longer hear them, he stretched out his long slender tail and felt about with its sensitive tip. No Ee-nie, Me-nie, or Mi-nie could he feel. "They've stopped on the way," he told himself and left me to go on after the cheese crumbs alone."*

You are the artist, you decide.

A participation form is in back. You may submit a photo-copy. Read, understand, sign, and enclose the participation fee. Or, enter online at

www.aedok.com/graymouseartsearch

Have fun. We look forward to receiving your creations.

way he sliced out a large chunk. By heaving and tugging it was all he could manage to lug it across the open space. Ee-nie, Me-nie, and Mi-nie, he thought, should be there to help him with it. Where were they, he began to wonder. Why hadn't they caught up with him?

Then he heard a scurrying of tiny feet and the piercing squeak . . . their signal. Mo dropped the piece of cheese he was carrying and peered around the edge of the cheese-cut in the direction of the hubbub. He was just in time to see Ee-nie, Me-nie, and Mi-nie disappearing around a huge brown teapot. Only by inches did they escape a great cushiony foot of the Meow with claws reaching out to hook them. The Meow was after them for sure.

Down crouched Mo trying to look like nothing in particular. But in a moment he was up again. He realized he couldn't fool the Meow that way. Ee-nie, Me-nie, and Mi-nie had found a hideaway behind the big brown teapot. If he could only reach there too!

It was no use. Bam! The Meow's big cushiony foot landed on Mo's back. It squashed him onto the shelf as flat as a pancake.

Mo let out one despairing squeak, then lay still. There was no use trying to wiggle or squirm his way out from under that heavy foot. He'd wait. He waited and he waited. It seemed to him he'd waited a long, long wait when he felt the Meow turn his foot and hook a sharp claw through Mo's fur coat and lift him up high. When Mo dared open his eyes which he had kept tightly closed while the foot was carrying him upward, he gazed into the Meow's great green eyes which, blazing with excitement, were examining him closely. Then as he usually did when he caught a mouse, the Meow tossed Mo into the air. Up, Up, went Mo, high above the Meow's head.

Mo knew that whatever goes up must come down and looking down as he was going up he could see the Meow's wide open jaws waiting to catch him when he dropped. Icy shivers ran up and down his backbone under his fur coat. He knew he'd be a goner if he dropped into those jaws. He'd have to think quickly if he was going to save his life. He didn't waste any time but quick as a flash thought, "I passed a wash line as I was coming up . . . too high for the Meow to reach. I'll flop over in a double somersault, give my body a sideways twist, and catch that wash line on

THIS IS
PICTURE PAGE 29

The information provided on this page will not appear in the 8.5" x 11" full color Picture Book. This page will be a single piece of artwork. It will be 8.5" x 11" glossy, full color.

THE THEME OF *THIS* PICTURE PAGE
Mo The Pancake

AEDOK recommends the theme of this PICTURE PAGE be based upon this text from the previous page:

> *It was no use. Bam! The Meow's big cushiony foot landed on Mo's back. It squashed him onto the shelf as flat as a pancake.*

You are the artist, you decide.

A participation form is in back. You may submit a photo-copy. Read, understand, sign, and enclose the participation fee. Or, enter online at

www.aedok.com/graymouseartsearch

Have fun. We look forward to receiving your creations.

my way down. Once I get my balance on that line I can stay there and escape that terrible open cavern filled with sharp teeth that are waiting to crunch me into little bits."

So Mo did just what he thought he'd do. He caught the line, hung upside down for a second, righted himself, balanced on the swaying rope, then like a rope walker at the circus, ran to the end. *But at the end, there was nothing for him to step onto. Back to the other end of the rope he ran. Nothing there either . . . nothing but the nail that held the rope to the wall and that was too small for him to step onto.*

Beneath him the Meow growled with rage, yowled, "Me-owo-wow," and spit, "Pish! Pish! Pish!" hopping about as though he were on a hot griddle as he followed Mo who kept running from one end of the wash-rope to the other.

It took a lot of muscle to balance on the wasp-rope and Mo's legs soon began to wobble loosely. Just when he was sure he'd topple off and go tumbling down into the Meow's mouth with those terrifying teeth, advice came to him from Ee-nie, Me-nie, and Mi-nie hidden away behind the brown teapot.

"Mo! Oh, Mo!" they squeaked, "Jump to the pan of milk on the shelf."

Mo looked at the shelf. Could he make such a long jump, tired as he was?

The Meow quickly turned his head around on his neck to see where those warning squeaks had come from. "What goes on?" he cried?" twisting his body after his head. And Mo, afraid that the Meow would follow those squeaks and find Ee-nie, Me-nie, and Mi-nie to their hideaway, diverted his attention by making a spring that landed him *on* the meow's head smack behind the ears. Up rose the Meow's tail, up rose his backbone too in a hump, he was so taken by surprise. And over that backbone hump ran Mo. And up the tail he crawled. From there to the shelf was no jump at all. But, the pan of milk barred his way. There was no getting by it so up on the edge of it he swung himself and into the milk he dived and swam for the farther side.

The Meow was almost as quick as Mo. Down he dropped his back, but by that time Mo was crawling up his tail. Down he dropped his tail,

THIS IS
PICTURE PAGE 31

The information provided on this page will not appear in the 8.5" x 11" full color Picture Book. This page will be a single piece of artwork. It will be 8.5" x 11" glossy, full color.

THE THEME OF *THIS* PICTURE PAGE
Mo On A Wash Rope

AEDOK recommends the theme of this PICTURE PAGE be based upon this text from the previous page:

> *But at the end, there was nothing for him to step onto. Back to the other end of the rope he ran. Nothing there either . . . nothing but the nail that held the rope to the wall and that was too small for him to step onto.*

> *Beneath him the Meow growled with rage, yowled, "Me-owo-wow," and spit, "Pish! Pish! Pish!" hopping about as though he were on a hot griddle as he followed Mo who kept running from one end of the wash-rope to the other.*

You are the artist, you decide.

A participation form is in back. You may submit a photo-copy. Read, understand, sign, and enclose the participation fee. Or, enter online at

www.aedok.com/graymouseartsearch

Have fun. We look forward to receiving your creations.

but by then Mo was swimming through the milk. *Out he reached one of his big cushiony feet and grasped the nearby edge of the milk pan. He came down so hard on it that it tipped toward him and slop, slop, slop, the milk slipped out, splashed into the Meow's eyes and dripped off his nose.*

Now as the milk ran out onto the Meow, it left Mo in the center of the moist pan slanting up on one side and with no milk to swim in. Frantically Mo tried to clamor up the inclined surface but every time he crept ahead he slipped back nearer the greedy green-eyed milk splashed Meow, peering up at him from below.

"Sideways, sideways, sideways," squeaked Ee-nie, Me-nie, and Mi-nie all together. And Mo set all four of his feet working sideways like a crab and sidled up to the farther rim of the milk pan.

The Meow took his outstretched foot from the milk pan to wipe the milk from his nose and chin and Mo leaped over the milk pan's rim and scurried along the shelf in search of a out-going hole to bob into. This way and that he looked. There wasn't a hole anywhere. But he did see a tuft of paper sticking out where he knew a hole had been. He couldn't get out of the Pantry Shop the way he had come in for he'd have to cross the Pantry Shop floor and the Meow could surely catch him there. The Meow was already reaching for him again and there was nothing for Mo to do but squeeze in behind the tuft of paper that had been pushed the going-out hole.

Mo was sure the Meow couldn't see him there for he himself couldn't see the Meow for the paper spread out so far and covered up even his tail. Never once did he think of the tell-tale dib-dab toe marks he had made of milk across the shelf when he was getting where he was.

Those mouse tracks did not escape the Meow's keen green eyes. He knew where Mo was hiding and over toward him he slyly crept, slinking along until he was close to the paper plug. Then out went his foot with sharp claws extended and quickly he jabbed the paper plug. His intention was to pull the paper away so it could no longer give Mo protection. And this time he'd waste no time playing with him but gobble him up in one bite.

But the Meow had used too much strength in his jab. His claws were caught fast in the paper and he could not drag them away. He gave a

THIS IS
PICTURE PAGE 33

The information provided on this page will not appear in the 8.5" x 11" full color Picture Book. This page will be a single piece of artwork. It will be 8.5" x 11" glossy, full color.

THE THEME OF *THIS* PICTURE PAGE
Sloshing Milk

AEDOK recommends the theme of this PICTURE PAGE be based upon this text from the previous page:

> *Out he reached one of his big cushiony feet and grasped the nearby edge of the milk pan. He came down so hard on it that it tipped toward him and slop, slop, slop, the milk slipped out, splashed into the Meow's eyes and dripped off his nose.*

You are the artist, you decide.

A participation form is in back. You may submit a photo-copy. Read, understand, sign, and enclose the participation fee. Or, enter online at

www.aedok.com/graymouseartsearch

Have fun. We look forward to receiving your creations.

great pull and the paper plug pulled out of the hole but still held fast the claw. Over his back the Meow rolled, snarling, biting, spitting, yowling . . . Me-owowowowowo. *And with his three free feet he tried to drag the claws of his fourth foot out of the paper plug into which it was fastened as tightly as though glued there.*

"Stupid, Stupid," *yelled Mo, jumping up and down in glee, "you've pulled the paper cork out of the going-out hole it plugged up and left the hole open for me to pop into . . . and so I will."* That's just what Mo did with only one backward glance. That glance made him so happy he couldn't keep from whistling a tune of triumph as he hurried into the passage for the Meow was still on his back and clawing desperately at the paper plug which still held the claws on his fourth cushiony foot.

THIS IS
PICTURE PAGE 35

The information provided on this page will not appear in the 8.5" x 11" full color Picture Book. This page will be a single piece of artwork. It will be 8.5" x 11" glossy, full color.

THE THEME OF *THIS* PICTURE PAGE
Mo Escapes, Bragging

AEDOK recommends the theme of this PICTURE PAGE be based upon this text from the previous page:

> And with his three free feet he tried to drag the claws of his fourth foot out of the paper plug into which it was fastened as tightly as though glued there.

> "Stupid, Stupid," yelled Mo, jumping up and down in glee, "you've pulled the paper cork out of the going-out hole it plugged up and left the hole open for me to pop into . . . and so I will."

You are the artist, you decide.

A participation form is in back. You may submit a photo-copy. Read, understand, sign, and enclose the participation fee. Or, enter online at

www.aedok.com/graymouseartsearch

Have fun. We look forward to receiving your creations.

CHAPTER 4

But after a while, the Meow eventually got rid of the troublesome paper, and went prowling about in and out of the Pantry Shop, hoping to find Ee-nie, Me-nie, and Mi-nie, for he soon saw the tracks leading to the teapot. But Ee-nie, Me-nie, and Mi-nie were no longer there. They had gone elsewhere while the Meow's attention was directed toward Mo and the paper on his paw. So the Meow kept on prowling.

Mo didn't know that. He went along the winding path that commenced at the open hole, merrily whistling because he wasn't worrying any more about the Meow. "I guess that Meow won't bother me any more," he said to himself, "I'm too smart for him."

So Mo forgot to be cautious and when he came to an out-going hole he made a leap without first looking to see where he would land. And what do you think? *He landed almost, but not quite, under the nose of the Meow! If he had hesitated, as he rightly should have done, and looked out of the hole before he leaped out so boldly, he wouldn't have leaped at all. But there he was outside the hole, shivering and shaking with fright, and wondering what he should do to save his life, for he could easily see that he was in great danger of losing it unless he did something quickly.* First he thought of simply popping back into the hole again but then he remembered that it is never wise to turn your back on an enemy. And he was a considerable distance from the hole, having leaped a great distance in his foolishness. But also, it was unwise to linger much longer where he was. He'd have to make a break. He'd dodge about until he could dodge out of sight somewhere. If he was quicker than the Meow he would be able to get in or under something.

So Mo began darting about as quick as a flash of chain lightening. And each time he darted here or there the Meow pounced after him. Mo was getting tired out and despairing of getting away when he spied a large red carpet sweeper. The carpet sweeper was standing still with its

THIS IS
PICTURE PAGE 37

The information provided on this page will not appear in the 8.5" x 11" full color Picture Book. This page will be a single piece of artwork. It will be 8.5" x 11" glossy, full color.

THE THEME OF *THIS* PICTURE PAGE
Mo Shivering In Terror

AEDOK recommends the theme of this PICTURE PAGE be based upon this text from the previous page:

> *He landed almost, but not quite, under the nose of the Meow! If he had hesitated, as he rightly should have done, and looked out of the hole before he leaped out so boldly, he wouldn't have leaped at all. But there he was outside the hole, shivering and shaking with fright, and wondering what he should do to save his life, for he could easily see that he was in great danger of losing it unless he did something quickly.*

You are the artist, you decide.

A participation form is in back. You may submit a photo-copy. Read, understand, sign, and enclose the participation fee. Or, enter online at

www.aedok.com/graymouseartsearch

Have fun. We look forward to receiving your creations.

handle propped against the wall. It hadn't any hole in it that Mo could see but it did have along crack all across its front. Mo measured the crack carefully with his eye and was satisfied that the crack was plenty wide enough for him to dive through without getting stuck halfway. So he gathered his two hind legs under him in a bow for a spring and then he straightened them suddenly in a high jump that carried him to the crack in the sweeper.

In went Mo, head first.

The Meow jumped too and came within an inch of grabbing Mo by the tail but being an inch short is as bad as not being near at all and so Mo was safe. All the Meow could do was to sniff at the crack and yowl angrily.

And that's what he did do, ambling up and down, now and then taking a long sniff a the crack. Every time the Meow sniffed, Mo moved a little farther back from where he was, until in a little while he was smack up against the brush that made the sweeper sweep.

The brush was on a roller that ran from one side of the sweeper to the other and from end to end it was covered with stiff, prickly, bristles. Mo lifted his tail and draped it over the roller so he could rest at ease while he was obliged to stay where he was. He had no more than got in a restful position when the wheels on the sweeper began to turn round and round, winding Mo's tail in among the bristles in a most painful manor. And Mo could do nothing about it because every time the wheels on the sweeper turned round, the bristly brush turned over and Mo went with it. Twice he had a notion to drop out of the sweeper and take a chance of scooting away, but each time he had that notion he changed it to a notion to stay in the sweeper as long as he could, for he could plainly hear the pat, pat, of the Meow's great cushiony feet. He knew by that sound that the Meow was following the sweeper where ever the sweeper went.

Every time the sweeper stopped rolling, the Meow put one of his great green eyes to the crack and tried to squint in so he could make sure Mo was still there. But always, before the Meow could get even a glimpse of Mo inside the sweeper where he was wrapped around the brush roll, worn and weary from so many times being upside and down, the sweeper would start on its rounds again. And, while Mo was in the sweeper he wasn't making any toe tracks outside of the sweeper, so that made it difficult for the Meow to determine just where Mo really was.

THIS IS
PICTURE PAGE 39

The information provided on this page will not appear in the 8.5" x 11" full color Picture Book. This page will be a single piece of artwork. It will be 8.5" x 11" glossy, full color.

THE THEME OF *THIS* PICTURE PAGE
Sweeper

AEDOK recommends the theme of this PICTURE PAGE be based upon this text from the previous page:

> *Every time the sweeper stopped rolling, the Meow put one of his great green eyes to the crack and tried to squint in so he could make sure Mo was still there. But always, before the Meow could get even a glimpse of Mo inside the sweeper where he was wrapped around the brush roll, worn and weary from so many times being upside and down, the sweeper would start on its rounds again.*

You are the artist, you decide.

A participation form is in back. You may submit a photo-copy. Read, understand, sign, and enclose the participation fee. Or, enter online at

www.aedok.com/graymouseartsearch

Have fun. We look forward to receiving your creations.

So after a while, the Meow got tire of trampling here and there on such an uncertain quest and went away to somewhere else.

And after another, and then another, short while, the sweeper didn't roll anymore. Something hoisted it up high above where it had been rolling, and before Mo could say to himself, "I wonder what is going to happen now," there was a creaking sound of hinges being opened up, then the narrow crack, through which Mo had dived into the sweeper, opened very wide and dumped everything the sweeper had gathered up in its travels. It dumped Mo out too, all wrapped about in a thick blanket of dust. The dust was very annoying. It got into Mo's nostrils and tickled terribly so that Mo had hard work to keep from sneezing, which would have been a dead giveaway to the Meow, if he happened to be within hearing. So he pinched his nose tightly between two toes of one of his forefeet and kept the sneeze from getting out. And while he was doing this he lay flat on his back just where the sweeper had dropped him.

He stayed like that for several seconds, not moving even an eye-lash. He felt black and blue and awfully discouraged. He guessed he would have to go home without any cheese for his poor weak grandma. And if he had to do that, then Grandma Graymouse wouldn't be able to walk anywhere at all.

He was thinking such sad thoughts when he began to think differently . . . the right thing for him to do was to get what he had come after. When that thought showed up in Mo's mind, he threw off the dust blanket that was wrapped about him and looked up and around. *But where on earth was he? On all four sides of him there were high, steep, walls.* It was going to be hard to climb out of such a deep down location. A trash bin, filled with pieces of wood and junk of all kinds. But Mo saw at once that such stuff would make an excellent ladder.

So he climbed on this, and he climbed on that, until he reached the top. Then he jumped. Fortunately he came down on his feet with no broken bones. He waited breathlessly for a minute with the terrifying thought in his mind that the Meow might have heard the thump he made when he landed, and be sneaking toward him stealthily. But apparently no danger lurked nearby. That was because the Meow was so tired from trailing Mo about in the sweeper, that all he could do was hobble back to the front door of the mousehouse on Wainscot Street

THIS IS
PICTURE PAGE 41

The information provided on this page will not appear in the 8.5" x 11" full color Picture Book. This page will be a single piece of artwork. It will be 8.5" x 11" glossy, full color.

THE THEME OF *THIS* PICTURE PAGE
Mo In The Garbage Can

AEDOK recommends the theme of this PICTURE PAGE be based upon this text from the previous page:

> *But where on earth was he? On all four sides of him there were high, steep, walls.*

We envision the view from the top down, to show depth and confusion.

You are the artist, you decide.

A participation form is in back. You may submit a photo-copy. Read, understand, sign, and enclose the participation fee. Or, enter online at

www.aedok.com/graymouseartsearch

Have fun. We look forward to receiving your creations.

and sit there to rest and wait for Ee-nie, Me-nie, Mi-nie, and Mo to come home that way. As if any mouse would be silly enough to try to do that while such a huge Meow was sitting where he was.

Now it may seem terribly foolish of Mo to go venturing back into the Pantry Shop where he had had a number of blood-chilling experiences, but he really was a brave little mouse, and cared deeply for Grandma Graymouse. So he said to himself, "Who's afraid of an old Meow?!" Of course, he looked around and kept his breath low-down when he said it. "Grandma has to have cheese and there is no one to fetch it for her but me." He clenched his teeth, stuck out his chest, and strutted away to find the whole he had come out of before he went into the sweeper. At last he found what he was trying to find and decided that if it wasn't the same hole, it was one that looked just as good, and if he went into it and kept on traveling, he'd reach the Pantry Shop some time, eventually.

And so he did.

Ee-nie, Me-nie, and Mi-nie were still in the Pantry Shop when Mo stepped out of the uncorked hole. They had been too timid to venture out from their hiding place and try to escape home. When they saw Mo they were delighted and squeaked their joy much louder than they should have done. "Mo, Mo, Mo," they squeaked, "where have you been?" And they ran as fast as they could to meet him. Fortunately, the Meow was to far away to hear them.

Mo told them briefly of his many escapes from the savage Meow, and then he added, "I'm after the chunk of cheese I left behind me."

So they all went together to the spot where Mo had dropped the chunk of cheese. But there was nothing but a grease spot where the chunk of cheese had been.

So Mo said, "I'm going to get a fresh chuck," and started away briskly to go after it. And Ee-nie, Me-nie, and Mi-nie went along too. Upon arrival, Mo cut off an extra large chunk of the deliciously odoured cheese and lifted it up as high as he could. The he began toting it along the shelf on which the main part of the cheese rested, going always toward the unplugged hole which they could dart into if the Meow returned. Mo, with Ee-nie, Me-nie, and Mi-nie following, walked slowly because the

THIS IS
PICTURE PAGE 43

The information provided on this page will not appear in the 8.5" x II" full color Picture Book. This page will be a single piece of artwork. It will be 8.5" x II" glossy, full color.

THE THEME OF *THIS* PICTURE PAGE
Children Are Reunited

AEDOK recommends the theme of this PICTURE PAGE be based upon this text from the previous page:

> *Ee-nie, Me-nie, and Mi-nie were still in the Pantry Shop when Mo stepped out of the uncorked hole. They had been too timid to venture out from their hiding place and try to escape home. When they saw Mo they were delighted and squeaked their joy much louder than they should have done. "Mo, Mo, Mo," they squeaked, "where have you been?"*

You are the artist, you decide.

A participation form is in back. You may submit a photo-copy. Read, understand, sign, and enclose the participation fee. Or, enter online at

www.aedok.com/graymouseartsearch

Have fun. We look forward to receiving your creations.

shelf was full of bulges made by this and that kind of dish and they had to be careful. They were almost at the end of the shelf, where they could jump off and scurry away home, when they came to an unusually large bulge. *Mo couldn't pass by unless he left the cheese chunk behind him and, of course, Mo wouldn't do that . . . not for anyone.*

"I'll cut it down to a smaller size," he told Ee-nie, Me-nie, and Mi-nie. *And so he did.* And tried again to pass the bulge. It was plain to see that passing the bulge with the hunk of cheese was dangerous. Every time he tried to do it, the bulge teetered and tipped forward at a frightful angle.

After Mo had tried three times to go past the bulge carefully, but without succeeding, he said, "I'm going to go past that bulge fast! Watch me."

Ee-nie, Me-nie, and Mi-nie watched. And they saw something happen that none of them expected to happen. Mo was right in the middle of passing from one side of the bulge to the other when over it toppled, flopping down with a crash-bang that could easily be heard from there to quite far away. Ee-nie, Me-nie, and Mi-nie were on the wrong side of the bulge. Mo was under its middle. And now not one of them could get a step ahead to go where they wanted to go.

"Come on, Mo," squeaked Ee-nie, Me-nie, and Mi-nie frantically, "Let's go back and hide 'till the noise fades out."

Mo didn't say a word. He just tried to do what Ee-nie, Me-nie, and Mi-nie asked him to do . . . go back where they wanted to go and hide. But he couldn't. Every time he tried to take a step after Ee-nie, Me-nie, and Mi-nie, his pink knob of a nose bumped into something that didn't seem to be where it really was.

After Mo had bumped his nose several times and it was getting quite painful and black and blue, he gave up trying and sat down beside the chunk of cheese.

"Come on, come on," urged Ee-nie, Me-nie, and Mi-nie.

"I'm a prisoner. I can't get out," complained Mo, "How can I come on?"

"We can see you plain enough." squeaked Ee-nie.

"I can see you too," squeaked Mo in distress.

"Maybe it's a magic trap," squeaked Mi-nie.

THIS IS
PICTURE PAGE 45

The information provided on this page will not appear in the 8.5" x 11" full color Picture Book. This page will be a single piece of artwork. It will be 8.5" x 11" glossy, full color.

THE THEME OF *THIS* PICTURE PAGE
Cheese Too Big

AEDOK recommends the theme of this PICTURE PAGE be based upon this text from the previous page:

> *Mo couldn't pass by unless he left the cheese chunk behind him and, of course, Mo wouldn't do that . . . not for anyone.*

> *"I'll cut it down to a smaller size," he told Ee-nie, Me-nie, and Mi-nie. And so he did.*

You are the artist, you decide.

A participation form is in back. You may submit a photo-copy. Read, understand, sign, and enclose the participation fee. Or, enter online at

www.aedok.com/graymouseartsearch

Have fun. We look forward to receiving your creations.

"It must have an opening," squeaked Me-nie, "We'll search for it and when we find it you can craw through." And so they searched. Ee-nie climbed up on Mi-nie's shoulders and took a look at the bulge's top side.

"If I see a hole up here, Mo, I'll put down my tail for you to grab and hang onto. Then I'll pull you up and out."

"When Ee-nie had examined the top, which was really the bottom of a glass bowl upside down, she said, "There's no hole, just a crack going downwards."

So Ee-nie got down off Mi-nie's shoulders and they examined the crack and found where it ended: a three cornered niche where a snippet of the bowl's glass had been broken out. Of course Mo tried to squeeze out through the tiny space the snippet of glass had left, but he couldn't. Then Mi-nie thought she had a bright idea, so she squeaked, "Put your tail out through the niche, Mo, and we'll all take a strong hold on it and lift up the niche so it will be bigger and you can back out hind-side-to."

So Mo got up and put his tail out through the niche. And Ee-nie, Me-nie, and Mi-nie lifted and pulled and lifted and pulled, but they couldn't get Mo out no matter how hard they tried.

After a while Mo said, *"Give me back my tail. Your skinning it on the sharp edge of the niche!"*

So Ee-nie, Me-nie, and Mi-nie let go of Mo's tail and he drew it back through the niche to the inside of the glass bowl. Mo examined his tail closely. Where the sharp edge had pressed down on it, there was a tiny drop of blood.

"Just look and see what you girls have done to my poor tail," he said, *holding it up for them to see the blood spot.*

But Ee-nie, Me-nie, and Mi-nie weren't paying any attention to Mo any more. They were squeaking loudly, "I hear footsteps and I smell catnip.

It's the Meow coming this way. We'd better hustle home and tell Mama, Papa, and Grandpa where Mo is." And away they went. Mo heard the Meow's footsteps coming, coming, coming, nearer and nearer to the glass bowl, but there was nothing he could do about it except run around in circles and squeak shrilly in fear.

THIS IS
PICTURE PAGE 47

The information provided on this page will not appear in the 8.5" x 11" full color Picture Book. This page will be a single piece of artwork. It will be 8.5" x 11" glossy, full color.

THE THEME OF *THIS* PICTURE PAGE
Trapped Mo With Cut Tail

AEDOK recommends the theme of this PICTURE PAGE be based upon this text from the previous page:

> *"Give me back my tail. Your skinning it on the sharp edge of the niche!"*

> *So Ee-nie, Me-nie, and Mi-nie let go of Mo's tail and he drew it back through the niche to the inside of the glass bowl. Mo examined his tail closely. Where the sharp edge had pressed down on it, there was a tiny drop of blood.*

> *"Just look and see what you girls have done to my poor tail," he said, holding it up for them to see the blood spot.*

You are the artist, you decide.

A participation form is in back. You may submit a photo-copy. Read, understand, sign, and enclose the participation fee. Or, enter online at

www.aedok.com/graymouseartsearch

Have fun. We look forward to receiving your creations.

Yes, the sound of the toppling bowl had reached the Meow's sharp ears and he was on his way to find out what had made the racket. When he reached the bowl and saw Mo under it, he pounced as he let out a loud yowl of joy.

"I've got you at last!" he growled as he slapped a huge paw with all its uncovered claws down on the glass bowl, right over Mo. Mo stopped running and stood still, petrified with fright. Mo couldn't make a move.

But the claw filled paw never touched him. The Meow pawed and clawed and yowled and tried to bite into the bowl's bottom, so he could chew it away, but he couldn't even get a tooth-hold.

While the Meow was wearing out his claws and teeth on the glass bowl's bottom and trying at the same time to puzzle out the reason why, Mama and Papa and Grandpa Graymouse came to the end of their thinking spell. And they hadn't thought of one single thing that would put Grandma Graymouse on her feet so she could travel away from their house on Wainscot Street to some other place. As long as they had come to the end of their thinking, there was no use thinking any longer so of course they didn't, but instead they raised their heads and looked around to see whatever they could see. And the first thing they all saw at once was the empty corner where Ee-nie, Me-nie, Mi-nie, and Mo were supposed to be staying and playing. They looked once, then they looked twice, because they couldn't believe their own eyes. Ee-nie, Me-nie, Mi-nie, and Mo were no longer where they had been told to stay and play. Mamma Graymouse let out a loud squeak and began going around and around, moaning, "Where, oh where are my children?"

After a while, Grandma Graymouse raised her head and squeaked weakly, "What in thunderation ails you?"

"I'm worried," said Mamma Graymouse, "I can't find my children."

"No need to worry," said Grandma Graymouse, "they've only gone to the Pantry Shop to see if any one has brought in a new supply of cheese. I really need my cheese crumbs. I'm getting weaker by the minute."

THIS IS
PICTURE PAGE 49

The information provided on this page will not appear in the 8.5" x 11" full color Picture Book. This page will be a single piece of artwork. It will be 8.5" x 11" glossy, full color.

THE THEME OF *THIS* PICTURE PAGE
Trapped and Meow

AEDOK recommends the theme of this PICTURE PAGE be based upon this text from the previous page:

> *"I've got you at last!" he growled as he slapped a huge paw with all its uncovered claws down on the glass bowl, right over Mo. Mo stopped running and stood still, petrified with fright. Mo couldn't make a move.*
>
> *But the claw filled paw never touched him.*

You are the artist, you decide.

A participation form is in back. You may submit a photo-copy. Read, understand, sign, and enclose the participation fee. Or, enter online at

www.aedok.com/graymouseartsearch

Have fun. We look forward to receiving your creations.

"Oh, my! Oh, my! Oh, my!' squeaked Mamma Graymouse, "My children have gone to the Pantry Shop and I'll never see them anymore."

"Gone to the Pantry Shop!" echoed Papa Graymouse.

"Gone to the Pantry Shop." mumbled Grandpa Graymouse.

"Who gave them permission?" demanded Papa Graymouse.

"I did," said Grandma Graymouse.

And right then and there they bolstered Grandma Graymouse upon her pillow so she could hear better. They told her about the big fierce Meow.

Grandma Graymouse glared about at Papa, Mama, and Grandpa Graymouse angrily. "Why didn't somebody tell me so that I would know what danger lurked outside our house?" she demanded, and began kicking her feet around until the onion poultices flew off, scattering onions in forty different directions. "There goes those dratted, no-good poultices off my feet," she snapped, "I'll hobble out and bring my grandchildren back if it is the last thing I do."

Then Grandma Graymouse tried to slide out of bed but not having any cheese crumbs to put strength in her legs, she couldn't, no matter how hard she tried. So she buried her nose in her pillow and moaned and moaned and moaned, "My poor, poor, grandchildren. They're probably inside that fierce Meow that nobody told me about."

Just at that moment when Mama, Papa, Grandma, and Grandpa Graymouse were squeaking their loudest in sorrow, and the whole of the mousehouse was in an uproar, in popped Ee-nie, Me-nie, and Mi-nie, all shaky and out of breath.

"Mo's in a new kind of trap," they squeaked, letting their voices mix in with the hubbub. "He can't get out and we can't get in, but we can see him plain as day. We tried to get him out. We couldn't. Nohow."

"Must be a bowl or cup," said Papa Graymouse.

"How did he get under it?" asked Grandpa Graymouse, calming the others down until he got an answer to the question.

THIS IS
PICTURE PAGE 51

The information provided on this page will not appear in the 8.5" x 11" full color Picture Book. This page will be a single piece of artwork. It will be 8.5" x 11" glossy, full color.

THE THEME OF *THIS* PICTURE PAGE
Shock and Worry

AEDOK recommends the theme of this PICTURE PAGE be based upon this text from the previous page:

> *"Oh, my! Oh, my! Oh, my!' squeaked Mamma Graymouse, "My children have gone to the Pantry Shop and I'll never see them anymore."*

> *"Gone to the Pantry Shop!" echoed Papa Graymouse.*
> *"Gone to the Pantry Shop." mumbled Grandpa Graymouse.*
> *"Who gave them permission?" demanded Papa Graymouse.*
> *"I did," said Grandma Graymouse.*

You are the artist, you decide.

A participation form is in back. You may submit a photo-copy. Read, understand, sign, and enclose the participation fee. Or, enter online at

www.aedok.com/graymouseartsearch

Have fun. We look forward to receiving your creations.

"It fell over him when he tried to pass it's bulge with a hunk of cheese for Grandma," wailed Ee-nie, Me-nie, and Mi-nie, *shedding puddles of tears.*

"It certainly is made of glass," said Grandma Graymouse.

"Glass," said Grandpa Graymouse.

"Glass," Papa and Mama Graymouse wailed. "We'll have to go right away and see if we can move the thing and save Mo's life."

"But the Meow is there by now," sobbed Ee-nie, "We heard his footsteps creeping that way. That's why we thought we had better hustle home and tell you about Mo."

And then, after Papa Graymouse had asked a lot of questions about the best route and the best hole and just which shelf the bowl was on, and when Ee-nie, Me-nie, and Mi-nie had told him all he wanted to know, he said, "Ee-nie, Me-nie, and Mi-nie stay here with your Grandma, and we'll go fetch Mo back, if we can move the bowl."

"But the Meow is there," said Ee-nie, Me-nie, and Mi-nie.

"He can't get into the bowl, and he can't stay forever, so we'll wait for our chance to do what I intend to do, and let Mo escape."

THIS IS
PICTURE PAGE 53

The information provided on this page will not appear in the 8.5" x 11" full color Picture Book. This page will be a single piece of artwork. It will be 8.5" x 11" glossy, full color.

THE THEME OF *THIS* PICTURE PAGE
Mo Under Glass Bowl On Shelf

AEDOK recommends the theme of this PICTURE PAGE be based upon this text from the previous page:

> *"It fell over him when he tried to pass it's bulge with a hunk of cheese for Grandma," wailed Ee-nie, Me-nie, and Mi-nie, shedding puddles of tears.*

> *"It certainly is made of glass," said Grandma Graymouse. "Glass," said Grandpa Graymouse.*

If you haven't shown Mo under glass, now would be a good time as the family discusses his plight.

You are the artist, you decide.

A participation form is in back. You may submit a photo-copy. Read, understand, sign, and enclose the participation fee. Or, enter online at

www.aedok.com/graymouseartsearch

Have fun. We look forward to receiving your creations.

CHAPTER 5

You could be guessing for as long as a month of Sundays without guessing what Papa Graymouse had in his mind to do. But it was very clever, so I'll tell you what it was . . . and why he intended to find a knothole with no knot in it . . . and why it had to be the proper size for Mo and his cheese chunk to pass through easily, or it wouldn't be worth the effort of finding.

Of course, the Meow didn't know that Mama, Papa, and Grandpa Graymouse were on their way to the Pantry Shop. If he had, he would have waited right where he was and pounced on them, one after the other. All he knew was that out of the mousehouse on Wainscot Street a great lot of noise was coming. He picked up his ears and listened for part of a second, then he made up his mind. It would be much easier to catch one mouse coming out of a mousehouse that sounded full of mice folk, than it would be to get Mo. He didn't have to think twice on that subject. He stopped clawing the bowl, turned his heel and went out of the Pantry Shop *straight back to the front door of the mousehouse on Wainscot Street. There he sat down where he could watch and wait. He wouldn't have been contented to sit there so patiently if he had suspected there was another door to go in and out. But he didn't. And so it was the Graymouses' Lucky Day.*

Using their newly constructed back-door and the back route described to them by Ee-nie, Me-nie, and Mi-nie, Mama, Papa, and Grandpa Graymouse scurried along undetected by the Meow and found the bowl that had trapped Mo, and had no difficulty in seeing Mo under it, for it was crystal clear. Next, they went searching around on the shelf for the right, large sized, knothole with no knot in it. This was more difficult than one might think, because although there were many knotholes of various sizes and shapes, they needed one large and round enough for Mo to drop himself and his cheese chunk through. At last they decided

THIS IS
PICTURE PAGE 55

The information provided on this page will not appear in the 8.5" x 11" full color Picture Book. This page will be a single piece of artwork. It will be 8.5" x 11" glossy, full color.

THE THEME OF *THIS* PICTURE PAGE
Meow and Scurrying Micefolk

AEDOK recommends the theme of this PICTURE PAGE be based upon this text from the previous page:

> *straight back to the front door of the mousehouse on Wainscot Street. There he sat down where he could watch and wait. He wouldn't have been contented to sit there so patiently if he had suspected there was another door to go in and out. But he didn't. And so it was the Graymouses' Lucky Day.*
>
> *Using their newly constructed back-door and the back route described to them by Ee-nie, Me-nie, and Mi-nie, Mama, Papa, and Grandpa Graymouse scurried along*

Possibly an areal view of Meow in front and the Mousefolk scurrying along the back.

You are the artist, you decide.

A participation form is in back. You may submit a photo-copy. Read, understand, sign, and enclose the participation fee. Or, enter online at

www.aedok.com/graymouseartsearch

Have fun. We look forward to receiving your creations.

on a perfectly round knothole at the far end of the shelf, and began pushing the bowl toward it.

Mo asked, "What are you trying to do?" because he didn't understand why they wanted to move the bowl.

"We have to move this bowl that you are trapped under, over to that large round knothole at the end of the shelf," whispered Papa Graymouse.

"But why?" Mo asked, still puzzled.

"Papa Graymouse has a plan," squeaked Mamma Graymouse, "don't worry son, "help us move this bowl."

So Mama, Papa, and Grandpa Graymouse got on the back side of the crystal bowl and pushed with all their might, while Mo, from the inside, pushed on the front of the bowl. It was very difficult. Because every time the bowl started to move ahead, Mo had to stop pushing and turn around to pick up the chunk of cheese, and carry it forward. Then he had to set the cheese down and start pushing again. And, by now *Mo's front feet were covered in cheese oil* from carrying the chuck of cheese, so when he pushed, he would often slip and bump his *soft pink nose* on the inside of the bowl.

The bowl slid and stopped, slid and stopped, slid and stopped. And inside, *Mo pushed, carried, slipped, and bumped . . . pushed carried, slipped, and bumped.* But each time a little further the bowl moved. On toward the large round knothole at the end of the shelf.

After they pushed and pushed and pushed the bowl, eventually they reached the large round knothole, and pushed the bowl right over that knothole. Mama, Papa, and Grandpa Graymouse said in whispers, "Drop down through the knothole with your cheese chunk Mo, and scurry home with it. Go in the back-door and be sure you don't let the old Meow, who is sitting at the front door, see you."

But Mo had never use the newly constructed back-door. So he didn't know where it was or how to get to it. Of course he saw and remembered Papa Graymouse and Grandpa Graymouse gnawing away at it with their teeth earlier that day, but things look different from the outside. "Where is the back-door?" squeaked Mo, "How do I get to it?"

By now, it was getting late, and who knew when that sneaky old Meow would change his mind and start prowling around again. So Mama, Papa, and Grandpa Graymouse were understandably nervous, and started

THIS IS
PICTURE PAGE 57

The information provided on this page will not appear in the 8.5" x 11" full color Picture Book. This page will be a single piece of artwork. It will be 8.5" x 11" glossy, full color.

THE THEME OF *THIS* PICTURE PAGE
Pushing, Moe In Oil, Pink Nose

AEDOK recommends the theme of this PICTURE PAGE be based upon this text from the previous page:

> *So Mama, Papa, and Grandpa Graymouse got on the back side of the crystal bowl and pushed with all their might, while Mo, from the inside,*

> . . .

> *Mo's front feet were covered in cheese oil*

> . . .

> *Mo pushed, carried, slipped, and bumped . . . pushed carried, slipped, and bumped.*

You are the artist, you decide.

A participation form is in back. You may submit a photo-copy. Read, understand, sign, and enclose the participation fee. Or, enter online at

www.aedok.com/graymouseartsearch

Have fun. We look forward to receiving your creations.

giving Mo directions all at once. "Squeak, squeak, squeak." It was very confusing to Mo. It sounded to him like nothing but squeaks.

Papa Graymouse immediately saw the look of confusion in Mo's eyes. Quickly he raised his tail, as a mouse-sign of attention, and Mama and Grandpa Graymouse were silent. Then Papa Graymouse carefully gave Mo the directions to the back-door.

Mo said, "O.K." And down he dropped through the knothole.

Mama, Papa, and Grandpa Graymouse went the same way but more slowly. They were very tired, having done most of the pushing on the crystal bowl, and had to take time to catch their breaths as they went along. Also, they were not as young and spry as Mo.

But after a while, they got home and all the Graymouses were very happy to be together again. Mama, Papa, and Grandpa Graymouse, squeaking together, told the others how they had rescued Mo. *And then Ee-nie, Me-nie, Mi-nie, and Mo ran around center of the living room floor to play one round of their favorite game of Chase Your Tail.*

Then Mo presented three cheese crumbs to Grandma Graymouse who gobbled them up the instant Mo carried them to her bedside.

Right away she said, "Mo, you are a hero!"

Mo thought so too.

Soon after Grandma Graymouse had devoured the three cheese crumbs, she said, "I'm feeling fine and as spry as a cricket." And she slid out of her bed, in a hurry. "Let's get going to wherever we are going," she squeaked.

But Mamma Graymouse said, Mo's tail is skinned in spots, so first I'll have to rub it with candle grease to keep it from aching, and then wrap a nice white bandage around it."

So Mo stretched out on the only table they had and Mamma Graymouse rubbed his tail with candle grease and tied it up in a bandage. After that, they were ready to start mousehouse hunting.

So they did.

THIS IS
PICTURE PAGE 59

The information provided on this page will not appear in the 8.5" x 11" full color Picture Book. This page will be a single piece of artwork. It will be 8.5" x 11" glossy, full color.

THE THEME OF *THIS* PICTURE PAGE
Playing and Moe On Table

AEDOK recommends the theme of this PICTURE PAGE be based upon this text from the previous page:

> And then Ee-nie, Me-nie, Mi-nie, and Mo ran around center of the living room floor to play one round of their favorite game of Chase Your Tail.

> . . .

> So Mo stretched out on the only table they had and Mamma Graymouse rubbed his tail with candle grease and tied it up in a bandage.

You are the artist, you decide.

A participation form is in back. You may submit a photo-copy. Read, understand, sign, and enclose the participation fee. Or, enter online at

www.aedok.com/graymouseartsearch

Have fun. We look forward to receiving your creations.

CHAPTER 6

The Graymouse Family of Wainscot Street was now ready to move. Grandma Graymouse had eaten her three cheese crumbs she needed for what ails here, the whole family was safe together, and they had a newly constructed back-door which they could use while the Meow sat at the front door . . . waiting.

Graymouses travel light. They don't need to pack bags. So out the back-door they scurried, down the alley that went by the back-door, mousehouse hunting.

They had just gone around a twist in that alley, when the Meow decided he was tire of resting: tired of looking steadily at one place in the front of the mousehouse. So he said to himself, "I think I'll look around in back, as well, and see what I can see back there." So he did.

As he was prowling about, with his keen green eyes he spotted the newly constructed back-door, a door that he hadn't know was there. Curious. And coming out and going in were plenty of dib-dab toe marks. Very curious. *But the tracks going in were all cris-crossed by the tracks going out so it was difficult to tell which way each set of tracks tracked.*

The Meow took a few long sniffy sniffs and decided that all the fresh toe marks were going in an away-direction. So he began sneaking along in that same direction, sniff, sniff, sniffing as he went.

Of course sniff sniffing a trail of dib-dab toes tracks takes more time than following the trail by sight. More time than he should have taken had he wanted to catch up with the Graymouse family. But the Meow didn't know that the Graymouse family had just turned the corner. He didn't know how old the toe-tracks were and he couldn't know how old they were by looking, even with his sharp green eyes. *He had to sniff them.* And, when he sniffed his nose full of one mouse toe-track, he had to clear the scent out of his nostril before he could take in a different scent from the next mouse toe-track, because mixing two scents together

THIS IS
PICTURE PAGE 61

The information provided on this page will not appear in the 8.5" x 11" full color Picture Book. This page will be a single piece of artwork. It will be 8.5" x 11" glossy, full color.

THE THEME OF *THIS* PICTURE PAGE
Just Went Around Corner and Meow Sniffing

AEDOK recommends the theme of this PICTURE PAGE be based upon this text from the previous page:

> *They had just gone around a twist in that alley*

> . . .

> *But the tracks going in were all cris-crossed by the tracks going out so it was difficult to tell which way each set of tracks tracked.*

> *The Meow took a few long sniffy sniffs and decided that all the fresh toe marks were going in an away-direction.*

> . . .

He had to sniff them.

You are the artist, you decide.

A participation form is in back. You may submit a photo-copy. Read, understand, sign, and enclose the participation fee. Or, enter online at

www.aedok.com/graymouseartsearch

Have fun. We look forward to receiving your creations.

is very confusing, even to a Meow. And meanwhile, the Graymouse family traveled very fast down the alley they were traveling, so they soon got a long way ahead of the Meow.

Of course as the Graymouse family went along they looked for empty mousehouses just as anyone who is house-hunting would naturally do. They looked first to the right and then to the left so they wouldn't miss seeing any empty mousehouses, and pass them by without stopping, and so this slowed *them* up too.

On and on they walked until they had gone about one mouse-mile, and there they came to a place that seemed to suit their taste very well. It had a neat little doorway, not too big and not too small, but perfectly just right.

"This will do nicely," squeaked Mamma Graymouse, so they went in.

"Comfortable," said Grandpa Graymouse to Grandma Graymouse, "don't you think?"

They were just beginning to make themselves at home, when Papa Graymouse thought of something to worry about. He had no more thought of it when he decided he'd better look and find out for certain whether he should worry about it or not.

So he looked out the neat little doorway they had just come in, and back up the alley they had just come down. Then he immediately called the rest of the family, in shock, "Look there! Look there!" And so they did.

And there they saw what Papa Graymouse saw . . . a long line of bare mouse, did-dab, toe-tracks, leading right up to their new mousehouse doorway, so that no Meow with half and eye, much less two good ones, could fail to see them.

"We can't stay here with all those toe-tracks showing just where we are staying," said Mamma Graymouse. "We'd better go farther, and find another mousehouse."

There was no arguing with that. The sole reason they were mousehouse hunting in the first place was because a huge Meow had decided to camp outside their front door on Wainscot Street. It would be no better to lead him or another Meow directly to their new mousehouse with a line of toe-tracks.

So they went out of the comfortable little mousehouse, back through the neat little doorway, once again into the alley, and started walking again. And when they had traveled a little farther, they came to

THIS IS
PICTURE PAGE 63

The information provided on this page will not appear in the 8.5" x 11" full color Picture Book. This page will be a single piece of artwork. It will be 8.5" x 11" glossy, full color.

THE THEME OF *THIS* PICTURE PAGE
Papa Sees Trail Of Tracks

AEDOK recommends the theme of this PICTURE PAGE be based upon this text from the previous page:

> *And there they saw what Papa Graymouse saw . . . a long line*
> *of bare mouse, did-dab, toe-tracks, leading right up to their*
> *new mousehouse doorway, so that no Meow with half and eye,*
> *much less two good ones, could fail to see them.*

You are the artist, you decide.

A participation form is in back. You may submit a photo-copy. Read, understand, sign, and enclose the participation fee. Or, enter online at

www.aedok.com/graymouseartsearch

Have fun. We look forward to receiving your creations.

another mousehouse. But before they entered, it was time for a family meeting.

"What should we do?" asked Papa Graymouse, "Any ideas?"

Well, they kicked around a few ideas, but none worth repeating, and then Mo said, "We'll fool that old Meow by covering up our tracks before we go to live in this house."

"Right," said Ee-nie.

"Where's the broom?" asked Me-nie, "We'll show that old Meow."

"We didn't bring the broom," squeaked Mi-nie.

"Mousefolk travel lightly," sighed Mamma Graymouse.

"We can each take turns in scattering dust over our toe-tracks by switching our tails over them," said Ee-nie, so proudly.

Grandma Graymouse just chuckled. And so they did.

Each mouse as he entered the mousehouse doorway stopped half-way in and half-way out, and switched his tail vigorously back and forth in broad sweeps. Back and forth, back and forth, spreading the dust about smoothly.

When this had been done by each little Graymouse in turn, they were all inside their new mousehouse and no toe marks were at their doorstep.

Grandma Graymouse said, "I'll make a cup of tea if there is any tea in this house." And she went bustling about to find the tea and the tea kettle, so she could put the kettle to boil and brew tea, if she could find any. "And I'll give them each a snippet of cheese for a surprise, too," she said smiling happily to herself, "Tea and cheese."

But then, "Oh, dear. Oh my, oh my," she whimpered and stopped still in her tracks. "We can't stay here either. We've only swept our toe-tracks off the front stoop. The other, farther behind tracks, come right up to there," she pointed.

Sure enough. Their idea was a good idea, but not good enough. Not a toe-track could be seen within a mouse-tail of their doorstep, but their trail of toe-tracks from the alley still lead straight to their doorstep.

"So they do, so they do," cried all the other Graymouses, "So they do."

"We'll have to go farther on and find another mousehouse. And we'll have to begin using our tails and spreading the dust all the way from here to there," said Grandpa Graymouse.

THIS IS
PICTURE PAGE 65

The information provided on this page will not appear in the 8.5" x 11" full color Picture Book. This page will be a single piece of artwork. It will be 8.5" x 11" glossy, full color.

THE THEME OF *THIS* PICTURE PAGE
Swishing

AEDOK recommends the theme of this PICTURE PAGE be based upon this text from the previous page:

> *Each mouse as he entered the mousehouse doorway stopped half-way in and half-way out, and switched his tail vigorously back and forth in broad sweeps.*

> *. . .*

> *Sure enough. Their idea was a good idea, but not good enough. Not a toe-track could be seen within a mouse-tail of their doorstep, but their trail of toe-tracks from the alley still lead straight to their doorstep.*

We envision last mouse switching back and forth, but still showing tracks leading to doorway.

You are the artist, you decide.

A participation form is in back. You may submit a photo-copy. Read, understand, sign, and enclose the participation fee. Or, enter online at

www.aedok.com/graymouseartsearch

Have fun. We look forward to receiving your creations.

"That's right," echoed Papa Graymouse.

"Not a toe-track is to be left uncovered between this house and the next house we're coming to," finished Grandpa Graymouse.

So off the Graymouses hurried, brushing the dust behind them with their swishing tails, leaving a cloud of dust to settle slowly behind them. It is good that no Meow was nearby for that cloud of dust would have been easier to see than the toe-tracks. But it did settle as they traveled along, leaving no trace of their path.

It was very tiring, traveling by foot and covering their toe-tracks that were behind them with the constant swishing of their tails. *But after a while, they came to another mousehouse* with a mousehouse door. They swished up to the door and skipped over the threshold. Then each Graymouse gave his tail a last swish and said, "I'm finished."

And so they were.

The job was done. There wasn't a toe-track to be seen from where they had been to where they were. But each and every member of this Graymouse family was now completely tuckered out.

"We'll have to find an easier way of getting rid of our toe-tracks," said Grandpa Graymouse, puffing hot and cold like a tired out old porpoise.

"The only way I can think of," said little Mo, "is not to make any tracks in the first place.

"What do you mean?" squeaked Ee-nie, Me-nie, and Mi-nie with excitement.

"I've been figuring it out in my head and I've solved the puzzle. If we wear shoes and have fewer loose toes, then we'll make fewer toe marks. A shoe has only one toe, but there is plenty of room inside the one toe shoe for all five loose bare toes."

"That's fine. Why didn't we think of shoes before? I think we've been very stupid," said Mamma Graymouse.

"But we haven't any shoes," sobbed Ee-nie, Me-nie, and Mi-nie, shedding great gobs of tears that ran out of their eyes and dripped from the ends of their noses.

"Well," said Mo, "the idea is all right, if we can find a shoemaker who can make mouse shoes."

"As long as I have lived," said Grandma Graymouse, "I've never known of a mouse shoemaker."

THIS IS
PICTURE PAGE 67

The information provided on this page will not appear in the 8.5" x 11" full color Picture Book. This page will be a single piece of artwork. It will be 8.5" x 11" glossy, full color.

THE THEME OF *THIS* PICTURE PAGE
Cloud Of Dust and Another House In Background

AEDOK recommends the theme of this PICTURE PAGE be based upon this text from the previous page:

> *So off the Graymouses hurried, brushing the dust behind them with their swishing tails, leaving a cloud of dust to settle slowly behind them.*

> . . .

> *But after a while, they came to another mousehouse*

You are the artist, you decide.

A participation form is in back. You may submit a photo-copy. Read, understand, sign, and enclose the participation fee. Or, enter online at

www.aedok.com/graymouseartsearch

Have fun. We look forward to receiving your creations.

"Neither have I," followed Grandpa Graymouse, "neither have I."

"Well, when I go marketing," said Mo, "I'll look about and find one. I'm tired of leaving dib-dab toe-marks, and having things happen that wouldn't be apt to happen if we had shoes and wore them!"

So, if any one of you who reads this story has any idea of where there can be found *a mouse shoemaker,* who can make mouse shoes of the right sizes for all the Graymouse Family, send word to the Graymouse Family on Wainscot Street because they'll be returning to their old home eventually, or send word to the publisher of this story.

THE END

THIS IS
PICTURE PAGE 69

The information provided on this page will not appear in the 8.5" x 11" full color Picture Book. This page will be a single piece of artwork. It will be 8.5" x 11" glossy, full color.

THE THEME OF *THIS* PICTURE PAGE
Mouse Shoemaker

AEDOK recommends the theme of this PICTURE PAGE be based upon this text from the previous page:

a mouse shoemaker.

You are the artist, you decide.

A participation form is in back. You may submit a photo-copy. Read, understand, sign, and enclose the participation fee. Or, enter online at

www.aedok.com/graymouseartsearch

Have fun. We look forward to receiving your creations.

THIS IS
PICTURE PAGE BACK COVER

It will be 8.5" x 11" glossy, full color.

THE THEME OF *THIS* PICTURE PAGE

AEDOK HAS NO IDEA HOW THE COVER SHOULD APPEAR.

It is totally up to you.

Decide upon a back cover that fits in with your front cover. It may be a sort of continuation of the from cover, or not. Some back covers are totally blank.

It depends upon what best fits into your artwork.

BUT REMEMBER. WE WANT THE CHILDREN AND THEIR PARENTS TO BE ATTRACTED TO THE BOOK.

You are the artist, you decide.

A participation form is at the back of this book. You may submit a photocopy if you don't want to damage this book to remove the form. Read the form, understand it, sign it, and enclose the participation fee. Or, enter online at

www.aedok.com/graymouseartsearch

Have fun. We look forward to receiving your creations.

END OF BOOK

WHAT FOLLOWS NOW IS THE PARTICIPATION FORM.

You may submit a photo-copy if you don't want to damage this book to remove the form. Read the form, understand it, sign it, and enclose the participation fee. Or, enter online at

www.aedok.com/graymouseartsearch

Have fun. We look forward to receiving your creations.

THE GRAYMOUSE FAMILY OF WAINSCOT STREET—ARTIST SEARCH
ENTRY FORM

AEDOK, the Archive for Education and Dissemination Of Knowledge, a division of
OSSC, Oklahoma Security And Supply Corporation
P. O. Box 161
Lequire, Oklahoma 74943
graymouse.aedok.com

Dear *AEDOK*,

Yes, I want to be a PARTICIPANT and submit my artwork in *AEDOK*'s *"Art-Search-Project for Artwork to the Children's Story THE GRAYMOUSE FAMILY OF WAINSCOT STREET"*.

I understand, that this is not a contract, that neither I nor AEDOK (OSSC) are under any obligations to perform, and either may terminate this arrangement without cause, compensation, penalty, or obligation. *I understand*, that I may withdraw my participation in this ARTIST SEARCH at any time without notice, compensation, penalty, or obligation, that these are rules that I must follow in order to participate.

I understand, that each PARTICIPANT must purchase a copy of *THE GRAYMOUSE FAMILY OF WAINSCOT STREET—ARTIST SEARCH* (such that each PARTICIPANT may have the complete text of the story and instructions).

I hereby state, that I have purchased and have in my possession a copy of *THE GRAYMOUSE FAMILY OF WAINSCOT STREET—ARTIST SEARCH*.

I understand, that in this ARTIST SEARCH, the term "PICTURE" means a work of art that is created by my own hand and abilities.

I understand, that all PICTUREs I submit become the property of *AEDOK*.

I understand, that I am required to submit 36 such PICTUREs.

I understand, that I am required to submit ONE PICTURE for each page labeled "PICTURE-PAGE" in the book *THE GRAYMOUSE FAMILY OF WAINSCOT STREET—ARTIST SEARCH*.

I understand, that each PICTURE is to represent the text of the story as presented in *THE GRAYMOUSE FAMILY OF WAINSCOT STREET—ARTIST SEARCH*.

I understand, that I alone shall decide what PICTURE best fulfills this representation.

I understand, that I may use Pen, Ink, Pencil, Crayon, Water Color, Oil, or any medium I feel most appropriate to represent my art.

I understand, that each PICTURE should be upon a sheet 8.5 x 11 inches.

I understand, that *AEDOK* in it's sole discretion, may enlarge, diminish, crop, or rotate the PICTUREs I submit.

I understand, that a PICTURE may consist of a sequence of smaller PICTUREs, called "SUB-PICTURES", to represent action or other complexities, at my sole discretion.

I understand, that if I utilize SUB-PICTURES, I shall do all the cutting and pasting, submitting, as indicated, a single 8.5 x 11 page for each PICTURE PAGE.

I understand, that I may submit these PICTUREs to *AEDOK* one-at-a-time (e.g. as I create them) or in groups, at my sole discretion.

I understand, that *AEDOK* shall upon receipt of one or more of my PICTUREs, place images of them on the *AEDOK* Website for the public to view and compare for the purpose of their expressing their opinion, by way of voting, as to which participant's art-work, PICTUREs, is most suited for the said PICTURE BOOK.

I understand, that there may be errors or omissions and I will not hold *AEDOK* responsible for errors or omissions in the placement of images on the *AEDOK* Website.

I understand, that images on the *AEDOK* Website may be smaller than my original PICTUREs.

I understand, that a visitor to the *AEDOK* Website may vote on individual pictures, or on groups of pictures, in a manor(s) at the sole discretion of *AEDOK*.

I understand, that there is a $1 non-refundable processing fee for each vote, to be paid by each voter, at the time of his vote.

I understand, that a visitor to the *AEDOK* Website may vote more than once and as often as he likes.

I understand, that as each PARTICIPANT finishes and submits more PICTUREs to *AEDOK*, and images of those PICTUREs are added to the *AEDOK* Website, an individual voter may upon review, vote differently than he voted before.

I understand, that in order to be a QUALIFIED APPLICANT, eligible to be selected as the artist who's PICTURES are to be used in said PICTURE BOOK, I am required to submit all 36 required PICTUREs to *AEDOK* by the submission deadline: Midnight, December 31st, 2017.

I understand, that should I fail to submit the required 36 pictures by the submission deadline, that my pictures can not and shall not be selected for the PICTURE BOOK, regardless of the outcome of the vote.

I understand, that voting shall be allowed until Midnight, January 31st, 2018.

I understand, that *AEDOK* shall be the sole counter of said votes and that subject to the other terms and requirements of this application, upon said count of votes *AEDOK* shall select the participant with the most votes as the artist who's art will be presented in said PICTURE BOOK (a $1500.00 value).

I understand, that in the event of a tie, the pictures representing the tying QUALIFIED APPLICANTS shall remain on the *AEDOK* Website for an additional month (until Midnight, February 28th, 2018) for voting to break the tie. And in the event of a second tie, the process showing the then current tying QUALIFIED APPLICANTS will be extended another month, and so forth until the tie is finally broken.

I understand, that I am encouraged to contact my friends, relatives, classmates, church members, organizational members, friends on the Internet, talk groups, bulletin boards, and others, to encourage them to view and vote often.

I understand, *AEDOK* will publish CD BOOKS containing the pictures of the remaining QUALIFIED APPLICANTS in separate CD's called *THE GRAYMOUSE FAMILY OF WAINSCOT STREET—CD*, one CD Version for each QUALIFIED APPLICANT.

I understand, that I will be required to sign a ROYALTY CONTRACT in order to receive a $1 per sale royalty on the respective PICTURE BOOK or CD version containing my PICTURES.

I understand, that *AEDOK* is not responsible or liable in any manor for errors or problems pertaining to the *AEDOK* Website, whether they be regarding images, or voting.

I understand, that *AEDOK* is not responsible or liable in any manor for errors or problems pertaining to the production and/or publication of *THE GRAYMOUSE FAMILY OF WAINSCOT STREET—PICTURE BOOK*.

I understand, that *AEDOK* is not responsible or liable in any manor for errors or problems pertaining to the production and/or publication of *THE GRAYMOUSE FAMILY OF WAINSCOT STREET—CDs*.

I understand, that *AEDOK*, at its sole discretion, may discontinue production, publication, and/or sale of *THE GRAYMOUSE FAMILY OF WAINSCOT STREET—PICTURE BOOK* at any time without prior notice, and without penalty or obligation, for any reason deemed sufficient to *AEDOK*.

I understand, that *AEDOK*, at its sole discretion, may discontinue production, publication, and/or sale of *THE GRAYMOUSE FAMILY OF WAINSCOT STREET—CDs* at any time without prior notice, and without penalty or obligation, for any reason deemed sufficient to *AEDOK*.

I understand, that there is a $100 non-refundable application processing fee (which covers among other things the cost of processing my 36 pictures, scanning them, and presenting them) which I hereby submit.

I state and affirm, that my participation in this ART SEARCH is purely for the purpose of SHOWCASING MY ART and that I do not expect or require monetary compensation of any form.

I have read and fully understand the conditions as expressed above and hereby request participation in the THE GRAYMOUSE FAMILY OF WAINSCOT STREET—ARTIST SEARCH, my non-refundable application fee being attached hereto.

Name (Please Print or Type)

Address (Please Print or Type)

City, State &Zip(Please Print or Type)

SIGNATURE (Required)

E-MAIL (a good idea to keep in touch)

www.ingramcontent.com/pod-product-compliance
Lightning Source LLC
Chambersburg PA
CBHW021002180526
45163CB00005B/1863